Contents

Foreword 7

Chapter One
"Your problem," said God, 'is that your mind is limited." 12

Chapter Two
Why we re-create God in our image 23

Chapter Three
Invoking God to smash into buildings and ride in tanks 35

Chapter Four
You're good and great God, but why all the mystery? 44

Chapter Five
If God's in his heaven, where and what is it? 53

Chapter Six
A pilgrim mourns: "It's hard to be serious about Revelation" 65

Chapter Seven
Does God choose Americans, Jews, Mormans, Notre Dame? . 86

Chapter Eight
Imagine a ball game in the sky 98

Chapter Nine
All right, God; do you program our lives? 110

Chapter Ten
The pilgrim grapples with how he prays 120

Dedication

This book is respectfully dedicated to Father Frank Mihelcic, the immigrant priest of my childhood whose sermons packed all of the suppressed tenderness of General George Patton chewing out a hapless subordinate: and to Presiding Bishop Mark Hanson of the Evangelical Lutheran Church in America. Bishop Hanson has tried to create unity among 5 million Lutherans, an act of bravery that qualifies him for early martyrdom.

Father Mike is gone. He was a man of apoplectic furies and wisdom, he taught me much and I loved him. Mark Hanson was my pastor for 16 years. He is a man of wisdom, high principle and nerve. He taught me much and I love him. Neither one would necessarily approve of some of the premises in this book. Luckily, I'm beyond the reach of Father Mike's thundering penance. As a concession to Mark Hanson, I'll volunteer 100 pounds of Jello to the next Lutheran pot luck dinner.

Acknowledgments

On a group tour of the Greek Islands two years ago, I would skip through the hotel lobby each morning to arrive at the dining room at the stroke of 6:30 a.m. for breakfast. Invariably Gloria Benson of Spicer, Minnesota, was already there, having persuaded the receptionist that the day was too glorious to waste standing outside a locked dining room. Each day Gloria and I got around to the mixed joys and bewilderment of faith. Out of those talks developed a serial seminar from Crete to Santorini, over cheese and pancakes, examining the airy possibilities of a private encounter with God. Some of that dialog has found its way into this book, and I relish the memories. In the midst of the writing I asked Joan Larsen of Chicago, explorer, writer, bibliophile and a wise observer of the human condition, to relate her visions of heaven. She remembered the reflections of environmentalist Paul Brooks, and, like Brooks, insisted that we can find a heaven during certain interludes of absolute serenity and wonder on earth. It's an idea that certainly deserves an airing. I want to thank Gloria and Joan, and also Jane Perry for her final readings—she who is one of the more ebullient Episcopalians I have met and a relentless sleuth for drooping participles, the misspelled word and wayward syntax.

With Additional Thanks:

The author wishes to thank Schocken Books Inc. for permission to reprint a passage from Harold Kushner's "When Bad Things Happen to Good People," published by Schocken in 1981.

The author also thanks the Minnesota Annual Conference of the United Methodist Church, publishers of the magazine "Northern Spirit," for permission to reprint material from an article by Sandra Brands in its issue of September-October, 2001.

The reflections of a correspondent of the author on the possibilities of "heaven on earth," contain quotations from the late Paul Brooks' book, "Roadless Area," published by Knoff.

The reflections of former Gov. Mario Cuomo of New York on faith and God's love are from one of the "Me and Mario" broadcast series produced by National Productions and WAMC Northeast Public Radio and made available on its website.

Foreword
Sixty Minutes with God

Of all the celebrities whose deeds and historic footprints have been plastered into the public domain for more than 3,000 years, the most defenseless is God.

Consider. God has been quoted, dissected, counterfeited and indicted on seven continents—each day for hundreds of years. He has been conscripted by military commanders and politicians to sanctify atomic bombs, and by meglomaniacal prophets to endorse homicide. He has been invoked by football coaches on 3rd and 25 and subjected to gender change by feminists. God has been confessed to and sworn at. He has been called omnipotent and pronounced dead, sometimes by the same people, depending on their luck at the blackjack table and the stock market.

To the best of my knowledge, nobody has ever made a serious attempt to get God's side of it. Job made a stab at finding out what God was up to, but Job was a chronic grumbler and you have to give him some slack in the field of reliable reportage. It's hard to lose 3,000 camels and maintain any kind of objectivity.

I'll confess never having heard the voice of God. I envy people who do. Most people who claim to have heard God make him sound like James Earl Jones doing a commercial in a wind tunnel.

Doesn't God ever whisper?

Does God sing? Does running the cosmos ever get boring? And if it does, how does God act in what the management people now call "real time?" Is he fed up with all of the images of God? Did he really tell Michaelangelo he blew it on the ceiling of the Sistine Chapel?

And is he the God idealized both in mythology and the lives of billions of people on earth today? If he is, why is there so much violence, hatred and hunger in the world today? Is it part of God's blueprint for our lives and the earth, this apparent passivity in the face of grief? And if we are bewildered by the paradox of a benevolent God and so much suffering, do we sometimes ignore the vast forces for good on earth?

The trouble with God is that he insists on being mysterious.

You could call it a quirk. One reason, I suppose, is that if he weren't so hard to track and comprehend, millions of preachers, therapists and miscellaneous prophets would be thrown out of work and you would have a global depression.

My work for more than 40 years was daily newspapering. My personal life has been marked by relatively normal amounts of turmoil and joy. My grief and blunderings have been balanced by the gifts of some marvelous people who have entered and graced my life. They are people I've loved or whose counsel and generosity guided me. As a wanderer of a sizeable part of the world, whether trekking the high country or pursuing my work, I also made discoveries of the good earth that have lasted a lifetime. In my later years I experienced a traumatic six months of crises that brought me to a divorce, cancer and coronary surgeries and treatment for alcoholism. Out of all that grew a recovery of physical and emotional health and restoration of a faith that is good and sturdy.

It's a faith I carry each day but it's not likely to propel me to the nearest monastery or seminary. I'm puzzled by some of the odder sagas of Scripture. I'm irritated by the growing cacophony of voices purporting to be tuned to the will of God or presuming to be speaking as the agency of God. This leads me to a plain and rough fascination with how God reacts to all of this din. Since we are so insistent on imparting human traits to God the question is: does he squirm trying to figure out how to deal with (a) the doublespeak of some of those wonderful Biblical epics? and (b) with the mess he has truly wrought in creating humanity?

If, of course, he did create humanity.

I think he did, although possibly not with a puff of dust in an oasis in the desert.

I've spent much of my time running with the wind, a child of adventure. I climb mountains and prowl the earth, curious about what's around the corner and over the hill. In my ripening years I thought I'd try visualization. It's a lot more rewarding than surfing the Internet at two in the morning. So in this small book I visualize an interview with God.

It's hardly an original brainwave. Practically everybody has conducted some kind of conversation with God, stretching back to Moses and evidently including Pat Robertson. Mine is strictly make-believe, a benign and imaginary encounter that forces me to sift through some of my long-standing dilemmas about the shortest line to genuine peace. I'm sharing the dialogue with the reader in the hope that both of us might find ourselves inching closer to a reconciliation between our beliefs and our inquisitiveness.

Inevitably in the process I depict a God not as I imagine God but as I would like God to be—benevolent but testy in the presence of the grandiose or wrong-headed or the hypocritic; tolerant of stupidity but not of evil, wise yet in no way accountable for the misery we have managed to inflict on ourselves and others. I struggle with some of the legends of the Judaic-Christian history, as many do. So I simply air them out here. God either joins in my consternations, rips my logic or sometimes seems to be groping for a Higher Power.

I offer this with a sprinkling of mischief, the same kind that you may indulge when the subject is the Institution of God. In our worship or observance of God, if we had to pile into it the same relentless, round-the-calendar solemnity demanded by the gurus of salvation, God himself would have to demand a change of venue.

Most of the questions I have are real and sometimes painful to me, or continually unnerving. If God appears to be sidestepping some of them, it may either be a sign that he's even smarter than we think or the writer's admission that some mysteries are too good to be solved. You might identify yourself with a few or many of those dilemmas. If so, I'll modestly ask a favor: Don't leap to a conclusion that God's answers to some of these questions make him sound suspiciously like the pilgrim's alter ego.

If you are tempted to think that, it would surprise and sadden me very much. On the other hand, let's say you interpret this make-believe visit with God as one man's examination of belief in his passage into the later years of life. And God is invited to do the prompting and cudgeling and to keep the compass heading straight along the road. If that's your conclusion, I wouldn't be saddened at all.

I'll begin with Adam, but I'm not sure God did, which is more or less where the problem starts. So if you don't mind I'll revert to the church of my childhood and its summary penance of five Hail Marys for rash acts. Then we'll open the door to God.

Jim Klobuchar
April 2003

Chapter 1

"Your problem," God said, "is that your mind is limited."

God arrived for our appointment wearing jeans and a turtleneck. He noticed my twitch of surprise and waved it off, cordially enough.

'I should explain," God said. "Everybody has a different picture of the way I'm supposed to look. I came this way because you and I would have a hard time talking if I walked in as, well, a burning bush."

"Do you ever wear a…"

"A gray beard? Not on your life. I'm tired of that image and I blame the old Greeks. It goes all the way back to them. They connected long beards with wisdom, and I don't really need props like that. If God can't stay abreast of the times, I don't know who's going to."

God noticed my puzzlement. Here he was looking like a guy ready to do 40 pushups before lunch. He looked trim and had pleasant but unremarkable features that were—I don't how else to say it— timeless. He knew I had been expecting something overwhelming, a Profound Presence, possibly invisible, possibly soaked in incense.

"I don't want you to get the idea that this is some kind of disguise," he said. *"I don't have to do disguises. I want to speak informally, in what you people call the vernacular. Using everyday language doesn't mean we aren't dealing with serious matters. So we have to be frank. Although, naturally, I love you, I have to say this and I hope you understand I do it with absolute tenderness and good will: The trouble is your mind. It's limited. I have to take that into account. You're a man who wrote a lament years ago about 'how do you love an unseen God?' To this I have to say, 'I beg your pardon. I'm not on probation.' If you want the truth, I AM basically invisible. The American Indians have it about right. I move with the sky and the wind. I'm everywhere and I pretty much know everything, including the fact that if we're going to get anything out of this in the hour you're allotted, you have to put a face and a larynx on me and we have to talk. I'll try to be candid and patient, but to answer your first question, I never said I created Eve out of Adam's rib. That was some odd literary license that shows up in every edition of the Bible I've ever read, including the one being pushed by the feminists, who call me 'she'."*

"Are you?"

"Am I what?"

"He or she, both or either? Look, as you know, I'm totally reverential and respectful, but I'm here to find facts and I guess I have to note that you arrived here looking and sounding masculine...."

God peered at me closely, An unmistakable crease of disapproval formed in his forehead, suggesting that I should knock it off.

He said, *"Knock it off. We can get to that later. You need to know that I didn't come here to conduct a beginning course in anatomy. Where do you want to begin?"*

"How about Genesis?"

"What about it?"

"One of the first problems I have with the Bible is trying to find out where it came from. Millions of people insist that you, in fact—excuse me and I have to beg your pardon here. I want to be as respectful as I can in addressing you. By what name do you prefer to be called?"

"I think I said informality ought to be the rule. I'm more comfortable with that."

"How informal would you like me to be?"

"Why don't you try 'God.' That has a nice simple and quiet ring."

"Some people, God, insist that you dictated the contents of the Bible and therefore its every syllable is sanctified and contains absolute truth."

God stared at me with a careful kindness and patience.

"Be serious. If I dictated the Bible I would never have made a hero out of Darwin by claiming I created the whole world in six days. It was embarrassing to see that in print. Obviously I look at the Bible as a friendly biography. But between you and me, there's a lot in the Bible that I frankly don't understand myself. You take Genesis. I don't really know where they got some of that stuff. If you'll notice, there are two different versions of Creation. There's one with Adam and Eve in the Garden of Eden and another that totally ignores the Garden of Eden and that hairy story about the serpent and the apple. The frustrating part is that I was there when it all happened and I don't remember kicking these people out of Paradise. I don't remember talking snakes either. What made me edgy about the whole thing was getting into the middle of this brawl between the evolutionists and the creationists. It's still going on and it's nutty."

I asked whose side he was on.

God frowned. *"If I didn't trust your good intentions, I'd call that a trick question. The courts are full of second-rate lawyers who make a living on questions like that. It took longer than six days, I'll guarantee that. I don't know about the Garden of Eden, but it would have taken six days just to put up a cloverleaf on I-94 in North Dakota. But if you have any serious doubts that I created earth and all the heavens, you'd better fold up your Palm Pilot and walk out of here. Doing Earth was actually some of my best work although I'll admit I never imagined rocket ships and cell phones and electronic banking."*

"Do you think all those inventions are equally marvelous?"

"I think they're equally dangerous. They make it harder for the meek to inherit the earth."

I asked God if he thought up that original line?

"No," he said generously. *"I think I read it someplace in Matthew. To get back to how the earth was made, is there something you'd like to say about it?"*

I said I never had a doubt about who created earth.

"Good. All right, look at it this way: I created the earth but it took billions of years before it got into shape to struggle with humans. I had to do tectonic plates, Pleistocene Ages, volcanic eruptions, glaciers and dinosaurs and fossils, things like that. You don't do those things with smoke and mirrors, I have to tell you. I could have picked Mars. It was actually a close call. I finally decided it wouldn't be much of a life breathing red dust and trying to put out your garbage cans in 200 mile-an-hour solar winds. One consolation for me would have been that nobody who lived like that could claim to be the chosen people of God, the way everybody does today. So when you people start claiming to be angry with God and asking, 'Where is God when all of these awful things are happening on earth?' I have second thoughts about going the route that I did. Then I

remember that I am loving and forgiving, so I love and forgive and I just want you to know that you're safe from all those dippy prophets who keep predicting the imminent end of the world which, between you and me, is pretty much a loony tune."

"Hallelujah," I said.

"Well, thank you. You didn't really have to say that, although I always like to hear it. I'm on your side, you know, now and forever, as they say in the 8:30 services. I hope you don't mind my grinding a little on how the world came about. A lot of the scientists say the universe was an accident of nature. And to think these guys are actually tenured at Ivy Leagues colleges and get 25-page spreads in "National Geographic." Why should I have to argue with the scientists about how it happened and where those laws of nature came from? All of those block-long equations about time and distance and energy didn't suddenly materialize in a freshman physics book. I had to work them up before the Big Bang. I have to chuckle when I hear those erudite talking heads on television with their theories about how the universe came about. The way it comes across, there was some million-to-one collision of atoms and molecules and this got to be a critical mass and it all blew, and that's how it happened."

"Wasn't that how it happened?"

"Yes, but it was no accident. One of the biggest mysteries that people grope with when they think about the universe is what was there before the *universe was created. It's the same one they have about me. The theologians put it this way: I had no beginning and I'll have no end. I admit that's pretty overwhelming to the human mind and it even shakes me when I think about it."*

I asked if the theologians have it wrong.

"Not at all. That's the way it is. I am. I always was and I always will be."

I said that sounded pretty permanent to me and certainly would end all debate at our weekly meeting of the men's club.

"Well, it is permanent and I don't mind your telling them that it's indisputable. I find this no-beginning-or-end arrangement comforting. There's nothing very ambiguous about forever. I wish people understood that. It tends to give you a relaxed feeling about the future. So it's a lot easier to take it one day at a time."

I agreed. I had an observation. I said God and the rest of us work from different calendars. "One-day-at-a-time is a beautiful philosophy. But for us the days tend to peter out after seven or eight decades, after which...."

"You want to know, I gather, if there is a heaven."

I said we could get to that later if it was all the same to him. But first I had to say that I buy the Big Bang. "What I can't imagine, nor can any of my friends imagine, is what God was doing all this time before the Big Bang."

God crossed his arms, sighed and looked pensive, regarding this as a reasonable question.

"You mean all those eons before there was a universe?"

I said, "When courtroom judges take a case under advisement, they usually take two or three weeks, which can be an eternity for the defendants and absolutely hell for the lawyers. But eons, God. What were you doing all of those eons when everything around you was essentially...."

"Essentially nothing? Bottomless? The mother of all black holes? Is that the suggestion?""

I offered my modest compliments to God on his active rhetoric. "Yes," I said, "basically that."

God smiled benevolently, forgiving my primitive ignorance.

"I suppose you could argue that, being God, I'd need only split seconds to produce that complicated math creating the laws that would eventually govern all of space. But you want to remember that this was new to me like it was to everybody who came after. You think this business of light traveling 186,000 miles a second is something that came to me off the wall? It's not something you dream up and just wing it. When kids today tell you that the sun is 93 million miles from the earth, you better believe the earth didn't just blunder into that. I had to fine tune it so that people could live in northern Minnesota, for example, on days when it got as low as 40 below

zero. But if I put the earth a million miles further out, you know what you'd have in northern Minnesota, don't you?"

"The mother of all school closings," I guessed.

"No. You'd have a frozen Sahara from Duluth to North Dakota, which itself would hardly be a magnet for summer vacations at 80 below with wind gusts up to 50 miles an hour. In other words the earth's orbit had to be so meticulously plotted that the earth would be livable at practically all latitudes and it would be possible for ordinary people to outlast or avoid aberrations like hurricanes, blizzards, tidal waves and armyworm infestations. Toward this end they invented vacations."

"And how would they be able to do all this?"

"With the free will and ingenuity that was their gift at creation, human beings eventually devised things like World Perks and time sharing."

"But none of this could be dreamed up overnight?"

"I don't see how it could. I had to calculate things like super novas and comets and wild card asteroids and the whole interstellar menagerie that everybody takes for granted today. I had to work the math faster than the biggest supercomputers. That was a major league mess to manage, all of those exploding stars and runaway galaxies whirling around in infinity. Which means that I spent a lot of those eons figuring the algebra for the Big Bang. When it finally came, it was a blast you couldn't believe and, of *course, it's still going on. The universe is young but the sun isn't going to last forever, and if you don't mind my saying it, you're not helping yourselves any by lousing up the ozone layer."*

I was glad to hear God talk this way because I had always put him into the environmentalist corner but suddenly we were swerving toward Endtime and I had to ask how long it would take the sun to start fading and for the earth to shrivel up.

"And while we're at it, God, is there really going to be an Armageddon? And tell me these Four Horsemen of the Apocalypse and all those trumpets and red dragons and huge beasts are the ramblings of a spacey prophet stressed out from meditational fatigue."

God sighed again and took on an otherworldly look of wisdom and compassion that, of course, surpasseth all understanding. And now this seemed to be a different God, I thought, mercifully liberated from our early banter that was calculated to put his marginally educated visitor at ease.

"*Look,*" he said, *I'll talk to you. But you can't expect me to tell you all there is to tell. To begin with, you can't really absorb it all. One of the things that makes people so fascinated by a power greater than themselves is the pure mystery of it. The unseen God you talk about. Is there a heaven and hell, and what's it like? Do you think I'm going to take down a whole industry—the spirituality industry—by telling you what it's really like and where and what is heaven, and if it is?"*

"All right," I said, "I'm willing to be overwhelmed. Let's start out by dividing the world into believers and non-believers."

"You can't do it."

"Why can't I do it?"

"Because half of the people who say they're believers aren't. And half of the ones who believe have doubts. Like you."

"I believe," I said.

"You believe there is somebody or something bigger than you, who set all this in motion and is loving and benevolent and forgiving, and like that. You believe that because life doesn't make sense to you if there isn't such a being, something that began all of it, and gave life, and manages to keep it together."

"Yes, I believe that."

"And so you pray."

"I do."

"Do you believe all of your prayers are answered?"

"No."

"Why not?"

"What is your question, God," I asked. "Why aren't all my prayers answered? Or why don't I believe they are?"

"Take it either way you want to go with those questions," God said. *"You probably won't like the answers to either one."*

"Well, how about a parable? If two of us are being chased by a lion, my pal and me, and we know one of us is going to make it out of the jungle, and we both pray, at least one of us is going to be very disappointed."

"This tells you what?"

"This tells me that it makes no sense for God to answer the prayers of one of us and to ignore the other."

"But some believers will say that there is a purpose to everything in life," God said. *"And the guy who lost the race served a purpose in being eaten by the lion."*

I considered that. "I think the lion could make that claim, but I'm not so sure about the guy who lost the race," I said.

"In other words...," God said.

"I don't think you put your prints on everything that happens in the world, God," I said. "You give me a will to decide how I want to live my life, and a conscience to know what's right or wrong. I think that is your will for me, to live decently and honorably. Sometimes I have ignored that will. But I have to say, honestly, that I don't think everything that happens in my life is a reflection of your will, or predetermined."

God's gaze fell silently on a large fluffy cloud floating distantly, and I would have sworn he looked troubled.

"You know," he said, *"I think I've made the point that mortals like you have limited minds. I want to be empathetic about this: It's right that you should pray, that you should believe in prayers. They can be beautiful. They define the relationship between humans and a nurturing power, a giver of life that is beyond them. Prayers ARE answered, although not always in ways people would like. I think it's fair to say that for every five mortals who renounce prayer because they have been disappointed, dozens more have felt comforted by the very act of praying, by their humility before something higher, and by their need. And whether all of their prayers are answered in some form, or some are not, I simply have to add this: You don't really expect me to unwrap all of my mysteries, do you?"*

God smiled.

What was I going to do? Argue?

Chapter 2
Why we re-create God in our own image.

"*You're a Christian,*" God said, in what I assumed was a gesture of providential etiquette.

I nodded.

"*I bring that up because you mentioned the Judaic-Christian Bible and I, of course, am familiar with it although I'd like to edit and rewrite some of it, which I'd rather not go into now.*"

"Why not go into it now?" I asked. And then I raked myself with a secondguess. Wasn't this rank insolence, trying to try to change God's mind and to invite some of his off-the-cuff thoughts about the biblical passages he admires less than others?

God showed no exasperation. "*I don't mind your asking,*" he said. "*I've never tried to discourage mortals from being free with their ideas and notions, no matter how far-fetched. If I did, Job wouldn't have babbled on and on about his hard luck. But to answer your question, I don't know how anybody would take it as a historic and literal fact that I turned Lot's wife into a pillar of salt.*"

I said it did sound like a rash act of petulance for what seemed to be a minor non-compliance.

"I couldn't agree with you more," God said. *"That part of the world around the Dead Sea has enough salt without me going into the manufacturing business. Actually, all she got was some short-term probation, although I'm not sure I want you to use that."*

"Are you saying I shouldn't?"

God pondered this issue. He said, *"No, I'm not saying you shouldn't. I don't know how I could listen to you praising God for the gift of free will and then slap a censorship on you. Another story that's puzzled me is Noah and the Ark. Now I'll grant you there was a flood. The archeologists will tell you that there were some big time floods in the Middle East thousands of years ago, but I don't know about this flood covering the whole world. All of this was said to have happened years into the time of human habitation, of course, because the flood was supposed to be an act of punishment for scandalous behavior by humans. I will stipulate to you that there was a lot of scandalous behavior—fornication, theft, usury, worshipping false gods, sodomy, blasphemy, adultery, hypocrisy, drunkenness, illegal immigration and all of the other usual suspects. But a flood that covered the whole world? You have to remember all of the mountain ranges had already been formed a long time before. If this flood actually covered the whole earth, it would have buried Mt. Everest under water and I think you are going to find a lot of yak herders out there in Nepal and Tibet who'll say it never happened and they never heard of Noah."*

God appeared imbedded in thought for a moment, as though something larger than Noah's Flood was occupying him, although if you were to track Genesis word for word there didn't seem to be anything much larger than The Flood.

"We were talking about other parts of the world, other people," he said. *"You know, millions of people call me Allah."*

I said I was aware of that. "You seem disturbed," I said.

"I'm not disturbed at all that different peoples of the world, with different religious creeds and histories, have their own names for me and their own concepts about how they're supposed to think and act to glorify God and to make themselves worthy. What disturbs me, why I grieve so deeply, is the terrible divisions between all of these people."

God did not seem to consider this an awkward moment, acknowledging grief so openly.

And then I thought this: Why should that be a surprise? As children we grow up being taught that we have been created in the image of God. And then for most of our adult lives, we reverse the process and try to create God in *our* image.

And who is our God of today?

The God we idealize today is a God of forgiveness, love, compassion and, when human beings slaughter and oppress other humans, a God of sorrow. Those are qualities desperately needed in a world where events move with racetrack speed and where the tempos of our lives are compounded by a technology that makes life more dangerous. Because of this, and because of our deeper understanding of the human psyche and emotional needs, most of civilization today is more sensitized to the power of healing and to the recognition of feelings. That is true despite the savagery of some of the events of the 20th Century and the new century. People long for a healing God, not a vindictive God, a God of reconciliation. We express that idea on our bumper stickers and in the hugs we give each other in church and everywhere else, including the checkout line at the supermarket.

"And you don't think those same feelings were there early in biblical history when God was being defined?"

I admit that the voice of God, right there, startled me. Then I remembered that God, being God, obviously is capable of reading the mind of mortals. Mine was, as he must have been telling himself, an easy read.

"And your thinking is that a different kind of God emerged in the older Scriptures, in what's called the Torah and thereafter."

I said, "Well, there were still plenty of affirmations of love, but I suppose when a one and omnipotent God was first being defined, the revealers felt they had to depict a God who sometimes sounded like the captain of the local military police or the provincial executioner. A voice of doom was a handy stage effect for the early prophets to shake the sinners into a repudiation of their behavior. So here you had a God who allegedly launched a global, take-no-prisoners flood, destroyed cities and threatened to kill children to the third or fourth generation for the sins of their elders. A punitive God, a vengeful God."

"And you didn't like that God."

"No. I didn't and I don't."

"Do you believe that was the way God acted in those years?"

"No."

"And you don't believe that those stories and characterizations were part of revealed truth in the Bible."

"No."

God raised some fissure in his forehead but, again, didn't look perturbed. He looked, well, intrigued. *"Do you care to explain yourself?"* he asked.

"What should I explain, God?" I asked.

"The collision between your faith and your skepticism."

God said it was okay with him if I attached no qualifications to my reply. The military code would call it "permission to speak frankly." I said the last thing I wanted on earth was to sound like one more amateur prophet, but I didn't see any collision between my faith and my selective skepticism. I said to begin with, I believed.

"Even without this face-to-face encounter?"

"Yes, of course. This entire encounter, as I tried to explain earlier, is freely identified as imagination *cum* reality for one hour. So I'm starting with the same blocks as anybody else. I believe. But killing children and wasting cities and crumbling the walls of Jericho are no part of the God I believe in and are incredible to me if I have to accept that as part of the God of my faith."

"And you decided that."

"Yes."

"What if I told you," God said, *"that all or some of those things happened?"*

"They may have happened, God, but I doubt that you gave the orders, or that anybody in your lodge gave the orders. In other words, the God that I understand to be the God of benevolence and mercy doesn't go in for genocide."

"So what are you saying about the different characterizations of God through the centuries, an angry, jealous and retaliatory God three thousand years ago, and today's God of tenderness and care?"

"I come back to creating God in our own image, or rather in the image of what we see in ourselves or what we think is good about us. I think it also is connected with the attitudes and character of the age in which we live. Most civilizations of today make an effort to care for the troubled and the underclass. Three thousand years ago the societies and ruling elites of the times produced whole constellations of gods. Ferocity and brutality were pretty much the standard social policies of clashing governments and cultures. It was altogether pretty barbarian."

"What did I have to do with changing that, if it's changed?"

"The Israelites found you in the midst of their travails. One God. Their prophets said you came to them and declared them your chosen people. Well, those were hard times, God. Those were the days of eyes for eyes and teeth for teeth. There wasn't a whole lot of mercy wasted on the battlefield or in the slave camps."

"Tell me about it," God said.

I blushed and asked God to forgive my presumption.

"Done. Do go on. I'm dying to learn how this is going to come out."

"The God of those times had to be a kind of tough-love God, if I read the books right. Barbed wire tough. When God laid out the rules, assuming the prophets got them right, the mortals who didn't comply really took it in the shorts when they went to the woodshed. They didn't get five Hail Marys in the confession box or, the way the Lutherans do it, an invitation to stand up in church with the rest of the congregation and say, 'God, I've sinned and the pastor will now make me holy.' In those days, according to the Scriptures, God didn't mess around being a fountain of compassion. If you were a mortal and you didn't comply, you got the BC version of the chair. Those were the times. The one God that I now know, the God we know, evidently survived competition with all of the Egyptian gods, the Roman gods, the Greek gods and, I assume, some of the Israelites' own candidate gods. At least this is what we're told in the old Scriptures. Which means the old Scriptures have got you making grim announcements, threatening announcements, telling the mortals to toe the line. You are quoted as calling yourself a jealous God. You are said to have wiped out all of civilization except Noah and his small brood because of the hell-raising going on in the world. That made you a punishing, wrathful God and, if you don't mind the wordplay, a nautical God. And that's the kind of God we see predominantly in the old Scriptures because God is supposed to have run the tight ship the mortals needed in that time of history. I grant there were times when God was depicted as an understanding and merciful God. I think Isaiah wrote some of the most beautiful hymns to God in all of literature. But you also were described as a raging God who wanted no gods before him. Today we don't want a raging God and we don't picture you that way."

"Are you finished?"

"Are you running the clock on me, God?"

"No, but you were going a mile a minute with those insights and I wanted to know if you were nearing a point where I had to prepare some kind of response."

"I would be humbled and privileged to hear your response."

"Let me say first that you may be on to something about the difference between the God of 3,000 years ago and today, at least how mortals look at God. I'm no different, but they do use different language today. Robert Shuler is a long way from Jeremiah. I'll admit that when I first read the Bible I was surprised by some of the things I was supposed to have said. Like the jealous part. I have no idea where that came from. I'm widely quoted as saying, 'I Am.' I may have said that because I really can't think of another way to say it if you ask me who I am. I'm alleged to have created all of those calamities to punish mortals, but if it went into a court of law I could probably put up a good defense that I didn't. I really don't spend a lot of time thinking about my image from eons past, and whether I was misrepresented or misquoted, which would not be the first time. I did face a lot of competition. I mean, there were Apollos and Zeuses and Dianas and Jupiters. They were all over the place. But here I am, and as far as I know, they're gone and they now survive only in those two-hour narratives by the tour guides in front of the Parthenon."

"It must have been a long journey," I said.

"It was, but it helped to have a fellow along like St. Christopher, the patron saint of travelers."

"But didn't the Vatican demote him 20 years ago and tell us he was a good guy but no saint?"

"You know, it did. There are days when I can't figure those people out. And the worst part was that I never even got to vote."

I told God I wasn't going to ask him if there is such a thing as Judgment Day. I said if there is, I wouldn't want to be the Vatican bureaucrat who defrocked St. Christopher.

God looked at me judicially but without reproach. I now KNOW I wouldn't want to be the Vatican bureaucrat.

Chapter 3
Invoking God to smash into buildings and ride in tanks

I prodded myself to remember that this was not just the God of Martin Luther, Thomas Aquinas and Jimmy Swaggert; in other words, not just the Christians. This God is worshipped in synagogues, mosques, gompas, sweat lodges and igloos.

"But by the way, God," I said, "how would you evaluate those three folks I mentioned?"

"I didn't realize this was a poll," God said.

"Call it a thirst for knowledge," I said.

"I'd say Thomas Aquinas and Martin Luther had their heads straight and created much good, although I didn't love the way Luther talked on the street. Also, he belched something awful, which I suppose could happen to anybody who takes too much German food. Jimmy Swaggert made me reach for a tranquilizer."

"So, everybody who claims to speak for God doesn't necessarily get gold stars from God?"

"Are you serious? I think Genghis Khan claimed to be acting in behalf of somebody divine. I know for sure it wasn't me."

"But there were people more recently insisting that they were acting for the glory of God, and some of them flew airplanes into the skyscrapers in New York and killed thousands of people." I said. "Where are we with all of these invocations of God by people who want to ennoble their acts of murder? I don't mean to confine those acts to the Islamic terrorists of our times. More important, where is God with all of this?"

Wincing and groaning are not acts of behavior that we normally attribute to God, but it probably is time to get God off the ceiling in Rome and down to earth. I would have sworn I saw God wince when we I got to wars and homicide for the glory of God.

"It gets terribly tiresome, if you want the truth," God said, *"people acting in God's name. You know it goes back a long ways. I was supposed to be on the scene when Moses and Aaron turned their rods into snakes that swallowed the snakes invented by the Pharaoh's gods. I mean, what was all of this stuff about serpents and how did they ever get me mixed in with a game of dueling rods and cobras?"*

I said it stumped me.

"I know where you're going, and I don't really know where it's going to end. I told you that a billion people or so call me Allah. That is their name for their god. Me. They recognize Jesus Christ and

Moses and Abraham, but they say I was revealed by their Muhammad, and they say that's the way it is. I don't want to parse all the conflicting claims made by the Muslims and the Christians and the Jews and the Hindus and Buddhists because there's practically no way I can do it. Sometimes I envy the Unitarians. They seem downright blissful without having to shuffle through all these emotional dogmas."

"But I'd assume that one of these is more right, closer to the truth, than the others."

"Well, yes and no. I don't have to tell you the circus Christianity has made out of what the theologians call pluralism, meaning differing viewpoints and philosophies. I don't just mean Catholicism, Greek and Roman, Anglicanism, Presbyterianism, Methodism, Lutheranism, Jehovah's Witnessism and all the rest. I don't see many people who are totally happy with any of them. People keep moving from one to the next like it's some kind of silent auction. I understand we get people in the hereafter who actually want to switch from one to another after they die, claiming their Sunday contributions to the collection plate were too high to begin with and they were misused to boot."

"But you don't restrict all of that intramural quarreling and hassling to the Christians."

"In no way. You must have seen all of those panel discussions on 'News Hour' during what you call the 'War on Terrorism.' They had Muslim experts and professors talking all about traditional Islam and

liberal Islam and theoretical Islam and your mind must have been spinning, because nobody talked much about what was happening in Saudi Arabia, where a lot of the violent radicalism was taught. And nobody was talking about Shiites and Sunnis, who were the ones on the ground—I'm sorry, that's the way they talk on American television. Anyhow, the point is that all of the religions on earth seemed to start with simplicity itself, with statements of principle and ethics and reverence for life and for God. And within a few hundred years they were at each other's throats. I don't want to be misunderstood. What I've said brings us to this delusion of 'holy wars,' and that's hardly limited to Muslims. Christians rode and slashed under the same kind of banner nearly a thousand years ago and with the same pretensions. The Crusades were a disaster and they probably should have been. The Catholics fought the Protestants in central Europe, Scandinavia and Northern Ireland and practically anywhere else where both of them figured they could spill some blood for the greater glory of God."

"Did you ever take sides?"

"I probably should have rooted against all of them."

"But what about these war cries in which generals and kings and presidents and dictators all claim their cause was anointed by God?"

"I haven't done one anointment yet. I admit it drives me off the wall."

"We say, 'up the wall.'"

"I know what you say. Do you mind? We have a different set of cliches in my world. The claim that God supports and blesses the warmaking of this side or that side is a fantasy that plays well on radio and television and in churches, synagogues, and mosques. The only one who seems to have a sensible handle on it is the guy in the Vatican, who keeps calling for peace no matter what the war is, and of course nobody listens to him."

Where were we here? Was God saying all wars, bar none, were without moral justification?

"I didn't say that. Some people go to war to defend themselves or to protect other people too weak to defend themselves. But usually there's a whole body of history tied into the causes of those wars, and unless there's a case of absolute aggression, a grab for land or power, there's usually a lot of gray in the responsibility for the war. The terrorists who attacked America claimed they were doing it because America had extended its power into the lands of Islam, which is correct, and that America was evil and demonic, which it normally isn't and certainly wasn't then. You have to assume they truly believed this. Their response was to murder thousands of people. Was the American response against the perpetrators' breeding ground in Afghanistan justified? Yes. Was it correct to call the terrorists' strike a jihad or holy war? You certainly never heard that from me. I don't sanctify wars. I'm too busy being called on to give blessings when they bury the bodies."

"Most Americans believe God is on their side whether they're in a war or in the Olympics. Millions of Americans have heard from the pulpit and the political stump that we are favored by God because our land is so bountiful and we're usually right in our battles and we also do pretty well in the stock market and the Olympics."

"Yes, I've heard that. When the Communists were in power in Russia the Russians usually won the Olympic games, and I can't remember hearing them give credit to God, although it's always nice to hear."

"So, you deny favoring this people or that people, choosing this people or that people, or siding with the Notre Dame football team."

"I do deny it. I think it's fine when people pray before a football game or a battle or before getting married. A lot of people could use providential help."

"The newlyweds?"

"Well, yes, but I was thinking more of their creditors. I hope you don't mind my small whimsies. Prayer matters. I know you understand that."

"I do. It matters to me, too. You've heard soldiers, athletes and a lot of people under duress simply pray for guidance, or pray for others, for the sick and lonely. Are all of these people truly devout? Are some of them coming to you as a last resort because they're afraid or alone or don't know who to trust?"

"That pretty much accounts for the bunch. Ask yourself a question? What category would you put yourself in?"

I considered. I started eliminating the improbables. And the more I did, the more I discovered something that hadn't occurred to me.

"I probably qualify for all of them."

"Yes, most people do. I don't think you have to make an apology. Tell me again what prayer does for you."

I thought of all of the times I prayed, of the times I'd been devout or afraid or alone or when I didn't have someone to trust; or when I prayed for someone I loved or for someone I thought needed love, or food or a friend.

Although my prayer was between my God and me, it gave me the warmth I feel when I'm in a community and sharing a burden or a joy or a hope. It took me out of myself. Sometimes it was expressing something from deep within my yearnings, something I hadn't shared without another person. Doing it, I felt unburdened and free of something dark and threatening. And then I would remember one of the axioms of recovery in the Alcoholics Anonymous program: 'You're only as sick as the secrets you keep.' I said, "I once was armed with a whole laundry list of appeals when I prayed, but I'd drastically reduced my list in the last few years."

"And what do you pray for now?"

I said, "I usually pray that I might do what's within my strength and energy to make life better for at least one person that day, to be as generous as I can, to minimize the times when I am rude, selfish or impatient, and for one more thing."

"Yes?"

"Each morning at the end of one of my small meditations I repeat a prayer I learned from a woman in one of my Friday morning meetings. I ask God to show me the way."

I paused there, remembering something.

"But you know all these things," I said, "why should I have to go through that whole drill?"

"Well, you didn't have to. But if you feel better for having done it, maybe you're closer to understanding the true power of prayer."

"That it makes me stronger knowing something about my vulnerability, it gives me a peace that at one time in my life I hadn't known at all."

"So whether you felt your prayer was actually answered, or heard, you felt closer to being the kind of human being you felt was God's will for you."

"That's true."

"I have one other comment. You said you know I'm supposed to have a reputation for siding with Notre Dame, and I also get that sort of thing from old grads of Southern Methodist."

"What's the comment?"

"Have you checked out the won-loss records at Notre Dame and SMU lately?"

I told him I'd rather not and, while I no longer worship with that church, I still root for Notre Dame.

"I know. I also hear your prayers on Saturday mornings."

Chapter 4
You're good and great God, but why all the mystery?

God said he welcomed my visit but he didn't want our talk to turn into some kind of progressive hair-pulling session where he'd be confronted with all of the wild suspicions and unanswered riddles mortals have about religion and what's beyond the grave.

I said I would hold my wild suspicions to the bare minimum. I further pledged that my approaches would be the model of civility.

God nodded, not totally reassured, I thought.

"Like a lot of people," I said, "When the talk gets around to religion I often go completely numb hearing all of the colliding voices claiming to know why God acts in the way you do, or declines to act."

"And how do I act, or decline?"

I tabulated.

"There was a calamity in New York in September of 2001 when terrorists flew airliners into the World

Trade Center towers and thousands of innocents were killed. Two years before that there was a massive earthquake in Turkey and thousands more died. There was genocide in Africa, absolute slaughter of more than a million people in Rwanda and elsewhere. It's gone that way throughout the world's history. Armenians slaughtered. Cambodians slaughtered. Civilizations torn apart by volcanic explosions and tidal waves. Mass death from famine and plague. Wars wipe out tens of millions."

"It's not a pretty scene, is it?" God agreed. *"Why do you bring it up?"*

"The enormity of it, God, both in the natural disasters and the cruelty that humans inflict on each other. I bring it up because when each occurs, there is almost always a response of incredulity from people who are devout. It comes especially from people who believe or want to believe but still have doubts. Those without religious faith are simply appalled in the face of disaster or brutality. Those who profess faith find themselves bewildered."

"A bewilderment caused by…" God said.

"By a single question: "Why does God let it happen?'"

"And what are the assumptions that lead up to that question?" God asked.

"The basic assumption that God is all-knowing; God knows all that has happened and all that is going to happen. And if God knows all that is going to happen or, more correctly, what could happen, then why wouldn't he intervene to prevent an earthquake that will or could kill 10,000 people? We would not want or expect God to stand by and look on when an army from one ethnic culture kills millions of people in another, people who are neighbors, living in the same country."

God was silent. His demeanor revealed no hint of judgment or suggestion that he was offended by the interrogator or by all those who presumably had asked the question through the ages. It was a hard question. It seemed implicitly to ask God to justify himself.

He said finally, *"I think one of the essential parts of a relationship between people and their God is a quality of mystery. I don't mean I impose a mystery to keep God aloof from people, that gray presence so many imagine. I'm simply saying what seems to me pretty obvious. People cannot understand all of the acts or inaction of God, how God works in their lives, because that must be beyond their comprehension as mortal and fallible human beings. Do you accept that idea?"*

I said I did.

"Then let me ask a question of you. You evidently assume that your God understands things that have happened, things he has made happen, and things that might or will happen in the future. Assuming that, what explanation do you have, if any, for God not intervening in those tragedies?"

I said my power to deduce these things was borderline miniscule, as God himself had suggested. But

I'd have to come back to the only way I can understand this seeming contradiction between a God of compassion and a God who 'allows' calamities like war, starvation, drought, and epidemics.

I said, "God is the architect of the universe and the creator of life. From God's creation, the earth evolved and humanity evolved.

"In its evolution, the earth is subject to the forces of nature—cooling, thermal action, the detritus of the mountain-building, erosion, climatic changes—the forces that produce natural convulsions. Having created the earth, God lets nature be nature.

"Having created life, God lets humans be humans.

"Years ago in the aeries of politics there was an expression, 'benign neglect.' It was one of Daniel Moynihan's marvelous manipulations of the language. It generally meant a wise and well-intended policy of leaving a messy situation alone until it got better on its own devices.

Floods, plagues and wars can hardly be called the results of benign neglect. So is a decision of God not to intervene in a developing slaughter the corollary of benign neglect? 'indifferent neglect?'

"No," I concluded. "The God of our life is not indifferent."

"What, then?"

My explanation to God may not have been very scenic, but it was the best I could manage.

God seemed fascinated by my philosophical tumblings.

I forged on. I said, "I needed to deal with a provocative view of God put forward by a respected and widely read rabbi, Harold S. Kushner, who has appeared on speaking platforms and in bookstores throughout the country. He has authored several books on our relationships with God and on the strengths available to those of faith. His most popular book, one that projected him into the forefront of writers on spiritual issues, was *When Bad Things Happen to Good People*. It was written, he said, in the aftermath of the anguish he felt in the death of his 14-year-old son, who developed an incurable illness as a child. The boy's death raised questions in the mind of this learned theologian not about the compassion of God but the actual limitations of God.

"A centerpiece of the book was his examination of the trials of Job, a good man who was apparently singled out for grief on a scale hard to comprehend—the loss of family, property, all he'd accumulated in a worthy life. There may or may not have been a Job, probably not. The story of Job, though, has come through the ages to symbolize to us (a) the unfairness of life, and (b) the indomitability of the spirit when it is nourished by faith and resolve in the face of suffering. In a dialogue he is supposed to have had with Job, related in the biblical Book of Job, God tells him, in effect: 'it's not easy being God, Job. If you think it is, try it.'"

My companion in the room was still wordless, listening closely.

"You've got to hear me through on this," I said. "It's the kind of mumblings a lot of people perform trying to get a grip on you."

God did not seem especially grippable in his silence. He looked amiable enough, even patient, probably wondering how this was going turn out.

"In the midst of his probings into Job, and into his own pain in the suffering and death of his son, Kushner follows the story to what seems to him the only conclusion.

"If God does not cause suffering, and if God does not load misfortune on innocent people, than why does it happen?

"God, he concludes, cannot be all-powerful.

"This comes from a respected man of God with a national forum. Does it make him radical? Blasphemous?

"Oh, I don't think so. It means he has thought it through in light of his own experience, and all of the unwarranted pain that has come to innocents in all ages, and in light of prayers apparently gone unanswered. From this he has made a leap of logic. He believes in a God as strongly before. But now he has decided there are some things God can't do."

"Is he right?" I asked God.

The silence remained unbroken.

I had to read from Kushner. "'There may be a sense of loss at this conclusion. In a way, it was comforting to believe in an all wise, all-powerful God who guaranteed fair treatment and happy endings. This God reassured us that everything happened for a reason, even as life was easier for us when we could believe that our parents were wise enough to know what to do and strong enough to make everything turn out right.'

"Yet the rabbi achieves comfort from his understanding of the limits of God.

"'Because we then know we can't be angry with God for our misfortune,' he writes, 'there ought to be a sense of relief in coming to the conclusion that God is not doing this to us. If God is a God of justice and not of power, then he can still be on our side when bad things happen to us. He can know that we are good and honest people who deserve better. Our misfortunes are none of his doing, and so we can turn to him for help...If we can bring ourselves to acknowledge that there are some things God does not control, many good things become possible. We will be able to turn to God for things he can do to help us, instead of holding on to unrealistic expectations of him which will never come about.'

"This, then, would be the God of guidance, consolation, hope and more."

God spoke, rather gently I thought.

"And do you agree with that perception," he asked.

I said, "I regard Kushner's perception as a brave one for the rabbi to have, and he had argued it with reverence and respect."

"But that isn't what I asked you?"

"No, it isn't," I said. "I wanted to give the man his due for following his mind and heart as truly as he could. But I can't accept his proposition. If God is not all-powerful and all wise, then it is hard for me to see him as God. And I do believe.

"I think God put humanity on earth. For me, evolution and creation present no conflict. So we evolved as we are today. We have the power to determine good from bad, to make decisions on how we behave. That is a grace from God. What we do with it is something God let's happen. Wars and epidemics and floods are part of life on earth. I don't believe God provides each of us a role. We do that for ourselves. Marvelous and ugly things happen as a result. Humanity makes dazzling technological progress at the same time that primitive people slaughter each other and misguided and hateful people assault innocent people. None of that, in my judgment, is the work of God or punishment inflicted by God. God doesn't prevent earthquakes or cause them. He chooses not to. Does he answer prayer? I don't think he's going to save the life of a dying old woman although millions may pray for her. I think the prayer he will answer is the prayer for personal peace, for hope, guidance and comfort and companionship. I know of recoveries that defy science. I believe there are miracles. I also think we often use the word 'miraculous' carelessly."

"And so you truly believe that if you are in distress or loneliness and you pray for God to walk with you, he will."

"I do."

God nodded. *"But you said you had another question."*

"I hate to do this, but what about that idea that God may not be all-powerful after all."

God breathed audibly and, I thought, wearily.

"Please," he said, *"one Job is enough."*

Chapter 5
If God's in his heaven, where and what is it?

I've been negligent in not describing the ambience of my conversation with God. Clearly heaven was not available. A man on a one-day furlough from the granaries of the American Midwest has to accept limitations. The truth is I didn't qualify for the throne room, and the other options, limbo and incineration, were unpromising.

God chose a small conference room of undetermined latitude and elevation. It had adequate furnishings—a desk, Gateway PC and Hewlett-Packard G85 printer, two softbacked chairs and a leather couch. A Muzzy system piped in pleasant and distant music, which God turned off after a few minutes, evidently not enamored of Mantovani's musical marmalade.

It wasn't heaven, but I had to admit heaven was on my mind. Of all the riddles that confront the pilgrim believers in their ponderings on life and beyond, the one that crowds the top of the list is: What's heaven like?

I looked ineptly at God. I say this because what's on my mind is usually no mystery to most of the people I know. For God, with all of his interstellar capacities, I was obviously a lightning-quick read.

"You're puzzled about heaven?"

"I am."

"Where does your puzzlement begin?"

"It starts with the idea itself. It's obviously no news to you that there is scant mention of heaven until very late in the Old Testament, and not much attention given to the hereafter by any name. The paradise of Genesis was supposed to be some place here on earth. So the Kingdom of Heaven is a late starter. By the way, there is still a debate going on among some of the Bible probers who insist on pinpointing the locale of paradise on the basis of the geographic descriptions in the Bible. Not everybody settles on the Tigris and Euphrates as the rivers of paradise. There was a scholar around here who said he had carefully done all of the calibrations. He said they convinced him that the two rivers that are supposed to connect with the paradise story are, in fact, the St. Croix and Mississippi of the American Midwest. I think he put the Trempeleau River of Wisconsin as another possibility in there. And the lush paradisian countryside was the Bluff Country of western Wisconsin and southeastern Minnesota."

God looked mildly surprised by this disclosure.

"You know, I hadn't heard that," he said.

"And by projection," I continued, "the scholar pinpointed the exact location of paradise as a place somewhere between what are now the towns of LaCrosse, Wisconsin, and Winona, Minnesota."

God leaned back in his chair as though mentally tracing the grid lines of his Rand-McNally atlas. He did not appear to be stampeded by this information. He did remain courteous. *"Please,"* he said, *"continue."*

"The scholar made the point that it was no coincidence that the country in question boasts some of the most productive apple orchards in the Upper Midwest, all of which might have been flourishing at the time of Eve."

"Did he say what the most popular apples are that grow there?" God asked.

I knew there was a God-the-Forgiving and God-the-Great but I didn't know there was God-the-Imp. I got the idea that God himself was baffled by the popularity of the Adam and Eve story and decided to make some mischief with the apples.

"Well, I don't know what kind of apples they grew in the orchards of Eden," I said. "Did they have Delicious apples at the time of Eve?"

"I thought you told me you couldn't buy the story of Adam and Eve," God said.

"I did."

"Why do you want to know the kind of apple Eve ate to get her in trouble?"

"Because I'm trying to tell you, God, that Adam and Eve and the Garden of Eden are fairy tales in my mind, but heaven isn't. You're the one who brought up the apples. God, there are a thousand versions of what heaven is supposed to be like. They cut across the creeds and myths of almost all of the religions. Look. Here were the terrorists killing people, American people, who the terrorists say aren't true believers. They have the idea that if they die while committing these murders, they will go to heaven and find 12 virgins waiting for them."

God interrupted wearily. *"The last figure I heard was 55."*

"Whatever. You must know that a lot of the old-time religion people still hold to those convulsive stories in Revelation, and the pictures of a throne in heaven and battalions of angels," I said.

"And you don't?"

I said it was a struggle. I told God I had trouble absorbing all those harps and white gowns and cumulous clouds that Hollywood loves to create from its digital arsenals to make entering heaven look like a walk into the Crystal Cathedral where Robert Shuler was doing the Sunday morning happy hour. It put a lot of stress on my limited mind. It made me feel like the best way to get to heaven was to win a lottery ticket on the Love Boat.

God closed his eyes trying to find a solution for this argumentative pilgrim.

"Are you sure there are many folks entertaining these same notions?"

I said I wasn't sure but it was a reasonable guess.

"All right," God said, *"If you think a lot of people don't buy harps and golden thrones, what do think heaven looks like?"*

"In most of my experience," I said, "people who don't see heaven as a floating greenhouse think instead of the times and places here on earth where they have felt themselves lifted into a euphoria. Not a spacey, goggle-eyed euphoria, but a manageable, relaxed and genuinely blissful state in which all tension vanished and all hostilities and anxieties subsided.

"I put this question to a friend of mine who tells of reading author Paul Brooks on the allure of the roadless areas. God, I don't have to tell you that this is serious stuff for millions of people who feel God's presence in the wild, or in a domesticated park or in the sound of swaying aspen trees outside a lakeside cabin. I'm referring to relatively ordinary people who don't climb mountains or make themselves hermits by living in a shack ten miles north of the last road to civilization. Most of them have a feeling that invariably grows into a conviction: that God is here in uncorrupted nature, gently sifting the stress out of them, making them feel humble but absolutely in harmony with the wind and stars and with God's spirit. And that puts them in the same community as the truly committed, roots-and-all nature-seekers.

These are the people who believe they can find God in a maple leaf or gliding under a full moon on a silent lake in the northwoods, and suddenly all of the distinctions between God and nature dissolve and for them God IS nature.

"I don't knock any of those, God. I fit into that community somewhere, although not always and maybe not quite."

God forgives eruptions of ambiguity. This I discovered right there.

"You mean you feel my presence in the woods but not in a muskeg swamp?"

I asked God to give me a little slack and he settled in his chair.

"My friend talked about the writer Paul Brooks' concepts of heaven. 'For him,' she said, 'it was somehow associated with wilderness. Heaven was not a garden or necessarily a Christian heaven with angels and billowy clouds. It was not even the paradise of monotheistic religion, since, ecologist that he was, Brooks allowed for the presence of mosquitoes in his heaven. For him, the afterlife lay at the end of a hard, three-day hike to a high, blue lake surrounded by snow-covered mountains. It's here that you strip off your clothes and dive into the lake. You build a fire and eat fresh trout, and you watch the gold of the afterglow on the snowy peaks beyond, and then you sleep the sleep of the righteous in this wilderness.'"

God gave himself a sensible time for cogitation.

"*Well,*" he said.

"I gather you want to know what I envision as heaven," I said. "But I have a question of my own. What do you think of needing mosquito netting in heaven?"

God said he was familiar with most behavioral styles in heaven but so far as he could recall he had heard of no one putting in an order for an unlimited supply of Off in the aerosol can.

"My friend is also a reader of the old Persian poet, Rumi," I said. "Rumi held out for a wilderness heaven also. He said the wilderness is a clarity of vision, a wide, select emptiness where, alone in the world, you experience a peace that passes all understanding. It is here that all of our questions are answered or rendered superfluous."

This authentically impressed God. He said, *"I like the idea of each person creating an ideal of afterlife based on an ideal on earth. Do you have an argument with that?"*

I said I thought all things obviously are possible if there's immortality after life is over on earth. "So if the greatest, most fulfilling time of your life was listening to the Rolling Stones in a concert in Grant Park in Chicago," I said, "you would have the privilege of doing that for eternity. Which, come to think of it, may be how long Mick Jagger is going to last after all."

"What do you think of that as a vision of heaven?" God asked.

"Compared with what?"

"Compared with mosquitoes."

God didn't give away much. What he wanted to know was whether my picture of heaven was something close to my friend's, something profound but notably not solemn, something that immerses us in the serenity and intimacy that flow from wild nature, immerses us forever. But I had to say that is not exactly what my friend imagined. Heaven might offer something like that, my friend concedes. But that image might be off the charts completely as a valid visualization of what heaven actually was or is. What she was idealizing were the truly wondrous moments or interludes of her experience in the here and now, experiences now graven in her mind. These are the moments or interludes—and most of us have them—which come closest to a heaven on earth, something sublime. And because we don't have a shred of evidence, beyond faith, that heaven is something permanent and good and right for us, then that sublimity we've experienced on earth may be as good as it's going to get. "The wild forests and high valleys, the mountains so magnificent that your breath is taken away," my friend said. "I don't think we have to wait and wonder about a heaven. I think it is before us, now, for those with the eyes to see it. It is really and literally heaven on earth. I want no more."

In this she may be a rarity. Most people see that experience as one that transforms them, one they will carry with them to their final mortal hours. But they want more of that, or something like that, in the hereafter.

My friend is saying that it may not be there in the hereafter because there just may not be a hereafter.

And I thought about it. But isn't that piling too much into a moment or an hour that brings us very close to the out-of-body mystique that the psychic explorers talk about?

I think so.

First, are there moments that reach that point of transcendence in our lives?

Of course there are. These are the times in experiencing a sensation or a rhythm of life when we are close to the enlightenment of the eastern prophets.

But then it disappears, because tomorrow we have to battle the freeway gridlock.

"Apart from the deepest fulfillment you've felt in a personal relationship," God asked, *"Have you experienced such unconditional joy as your friend described?"*

"The one time I felt very close to it in a lifetime in the mountains was a day on a mountain in Wyoming called Mt. Moran. Two friends and I were climbing toward the summit in mid-morning. I have climbed on more difficult mountains, and achieved the summit after hours of exhausting and dangerous effort. What I felt after those climbs was achievement and absolute relief. But on that day on Moran, while the rock was steep, the route was permeated with handholds and footholds in the hard granite, everywhere they were needed, whenever they were needed, they appeared. We were strong enough and quick. We could have virtually flown up the mountain. But we didn't. We moved easily and almost merrily. The sun was glorious on our faces and arms. We climbed without physical or mental struggle. Now and then one of us would sing. None of us had designs on La Scala, God. This was a song of simple exuberance and thanksgiving. None of us qualified as a superman on the mountain. But there are times when, for a few borrowed hours, your heart and blood can race with the wind and you can reach for the sun. And this was like none other. On the summit we wanted the day never to end. We were as free as the air and alone on the mountain and we felt, well, your grace."

God nodded. He smiled with a trace of appreciation. He said, *"And it was good?"*

"It was."

"And it stayed good?"

"Well, no. On the way down we took a short cut and waded through 500 feet of sunflowers. I had an allergic reaction that put me in the hospital for two days."

"And so that was bad?" God asked, evidently disappointed.

"Let's say it was, mmm, less than good."

God was on an interrogatory roll. He wanted to know first how I saw heaven, after all the ambiguities dissolved, and what about hell.

"I have a hard time putting a face on evil and calling it The Devil, although I believe sometimes there IS pure evil," I said. "I have to say I don't accept the concept of hell. I don't know if everybody who ever lived is ultimately forgiven and receives immortal life that is at least bearable. Some people who know far more theology than I do tell me that if you really believe, you accept the concept of God's grace; that it doesn't have to be deserved. And if that's true, they maintain, then you're very likely to see Adolph Hitler and Count Dracula sitting next to you in heaven.

"Wouldn't that be a scene? I believe in grace. I don't know about Hitler in heaven. I once talked to a minister whose own notions about heaven and the hereafter pretty much mesh into mine. I really don't know what heaven will be or if it will be. What I know about God in my time on earth is this: most of the time when I've been troubled or fearful and adrift, God has taken care of me. What I need to know about the hereafter is that whatever form it takes, God will provide."

Now it was my turn to do some mind reading. I suspected that God might be more sentimental than I am about harps being part of the hardware of heaven. He might have been more sympathetic than I was about John's cast-of-thousands choreography in Revelation. I really wasn't sure whether God was amused or annoyed by my expectations of the hereafter. But I heard no rebuttal. I did hear another question.

"Let's say you found moments on earth that seemed to define heaven, but you understood that they were fleeting," God said. *"Was there anything in your experience, a quality of life, that you would expect to find and hope to find if there actually is a heaven? In other words, where would heaven begin?"*

I said I thought it would begin where the best in humanity always begins, with the quality that gives life on earth its deepest beauty. If we can find it.

"And what is that?"

"Love is elusive for some of us," I said. "It is abused by practically all of us. We call a hundred things 'love,' and we tell so many people 'I love you' that we now use it on the mailman and the meter readers. But when it comes into our lives, and we give love and receive it without selfishness, it brings trust and thanksgiving into our lives, and it is like no other emotion we have ever felt. It is a commitment like no other, and when it fills our hearts and minds and bodies, we have something beautiful and enduring and at peace. It puts us very close to feeling an immortality of the spirit which, I suppose, is what heaven probably is all about."

God looked to be in repose. He had a last question.

"If that is so, why do you struggle to know what it feels like to be in heaven?"

Chapter 6
A pilgrim mourns: "It's hard to be serious about Revelation"

I didn't want to sound presumptuous by running God through the wringer of the "God Is Dead" theology.

God sighed. *"But you're going to,"* he said.

He sounded resigned. *"Spare me that, one more time,"* he said. *"Why don't we talk about something more palatable, like the barbarian abuses of the Spanish Inquisition? How about the witch-hunts at Salem? I can give you five minutes on Jerry Falwell."*

I said, in all respect, "We should get to that." But I had first to give myself some kind of framework for God's response to the discovery in the mid-1900s that he had disappeared somewhere in the fogs of mythology.

"I suppose I could stop you," God said. *"But go ahead and run it up...where do you run these things up?"*

"We used to say 'the flagpole,'" I said. "Now we prefer the Internet instant poll, the double-click method of finding out what America thinks."

I reviewed. When I was a young man the very idea that a God exists ran into an ambush from the reigning intellectual class. It was the pop-philosophy bombshell of the day, a noisy claim that God was history, gone forever. It made the rounds of the off-campus beer busts and the book-signing circuits and ignited a million indignant sermons.

'God Is Dead' was the rage of a new secularism that followed World War II. It pronounced an end to romantic notions of a supreme being who controlled our lives and kept a list of our sins and contritions. Like Santa Claus on Dec. 24 he would deliver a verdict: we were either going to spend immortality with the saints or in the sulfur pits.

Most of the 20th Century intellectuals had already said no to that scheme or had never bought into the God thing. But they were now joined by growing millions of main-street skeptics who rebelled against the fear-of-God preachments of their youth. They looked back on centuries of dogmatic beliefs in multiple gods, benevolent gods, evil gods, fornicating gods, gods of gold, of sun and darkness, and now a single god, and they saw no evidence of a god of any description running the show.

They could live eminently successful and loving lives, they said, without pretending that some invisible kibitzer in space was pulling the strings. God, in short, was no longer relevant. That was the proposition. Faced with this heavy-handed pronouncement, the liberal Protestant churches cleared their throats and said the debate on it was healthy and would give the Christian institution a sharper focus in how it teaches Christianity. Orthodox Jews and the Vatican met the accusation by essentially ignoring it. The "God Is Dead" phenomenon did not not exactly set off a global hurricane of atheism nor did it topple belief in God around the world. But it didn't blow itself out by morning, either. By the end of the 20th Century, church attendance in the United States as well as in many other western countries had declined seriously. But it wasn't only church attendance that alarmed the ministerial industry.

I was about to put these pricklesome matters to God as discreetly as my time allowed. "Obviously," I said, "the reports of your death...."

God moved in pre-emptively. *"Right. I'm still here. But I'm not as high and mighty as I used to be, is that the idea?"*

"I didn't use those words," I said mildly.

"But you were thinking that a lot of people have drawn this conclusion."

"Haven't you?" I asked. "I mean the evidence that people have slid away from God by the millions is hard to refute."

"It is, of course. But you're talking about where you live, the USA and other countries like it, where fast track living is in and the church-going believers are looked on as well-intended and vaguely hypocritical dinosaurs."

I confessed never having seen a hypocritical dinosaur.

God scowled. *"What am I supposed to do, take a course in composition? It seemed like a punchy metaphor to me. Have you got something better?"*

I said I liked it. And the last thing I wanted to do on earth, or anywhere else, was to edit God's expository style. "What happened," I said, "was that while I attend church on most Sundays, I've never seen myself as a hypocritical dinosaur. But maybe I am." I started to brood. "God, am I that far out of it?"

God decided to rescue me.

"You need to set the record straight. I didn't say you're a hypocritical dinosaur. I said the critics might look at you that way."

I said that didn't make me feel much better.

"The point I was making," God said, *"was that the practice of what they used to call old-fashioned religion has faded in some countries like the USA, although what some people call hard-rock evangelical churches are coming on in big numbers in some of the more prosperous suburbs. But if you look at the continent of Africa and other developing parts of the world, Christianity is making huge gains in those places. Right now I'll grant that religion is in a mess. Why would I deny it? I'm not talking about the abuse of religion by homicidal madmen and by political lobbies who generate millions of dollars to elect an American president. I'm not talking about radicals invoking the name of God to get even with*

somebody who stole five hundred miles of desert from them, and they want it back because they stole it from somebody else. I'm not even talking about the turmoil in the Islamic world over what Islam is all about. I do wish that when they figure it out they'd let me know."

"So, why aren't you talking about all that?"

"What saddens me more is the erosion of faith. That's different from church-going. The reasons why there is less church-going in America are not hard to understand. There's a whole grocery list of the ways in which modern Americans look for a spiritual life. They look for it in support groups, in meditations, on a mountaintop, in a birchbark canoe, in a hundred ways that seem simpler and more intimate and less expensive than by getting it in church. Then there are the young people. Most of them seem bored by the church experience or don't want it to cut into their Sunday morning sleep. But I see you rattling a sheaf of paper and you are going to give me some evidence."

What I'd brought was a copy of a United Methodist Church, Minnesota Conference, publication, called "Northern Spirit." It examined the basic problem of American churches today in the head-on style in which most churches whose eyes and minds are open. The magazine contained a report by the Barna Research Group, Ltd., which was identified as a marketing organization studying American churches and cultural groups. Its president, George Barna, wrote an analysis, describing the millions of

Christians (or former Christians) who don't go to church as "the unchurched." This may be one of the more ungainly words in the whole discourse on religion, but Barna makes no attempts at delicacy.

"They are not seeking more religious teaching because (having grown up in the Christian faith) they feel they already know the important aspects of Christianity. Yet we find that huge numbers of the unchurched believe that Jesus sinned, that the Holy Spirit is fictitious, that Satan does not exist, that there is no absolute moral truth (or) universal salvation and that all faiths teach the same basic lessons. They buy into some good perspectives...but their views are rather muddled and contradictory."

"Have you finished?" God asked.

I said, "Not quite."

"Proceed,"

"Led by the Baby Boomers, the report said, millions in the latter part of the 20th century developed a suspicion of institutions and began to accept the idea that life fundamentally has no meaning and that comfort and security are all you can hope for out of life."

"I have another question," God said.

"Certainly."

"When Americans were frightened after Sept. 11, 2001, especially the millions you call the Boomers, did they have the same distrust for their institutions,

such as the federal government, that they had before in this wave of rejection you're talking about?"

"In the months after Sept. 11," I said, "Americans thought the federal government was a wonderful thing to have around. By the multitudes they assembled in facilities called churches."

"And what had been their security in the years before that?"

"Well, probably their money and their lifestyles."

"And these were now threatened?"

"By an unseen menace."

"And so now those old institutions didn't look so bad."

"They looked," I said, "positively comforting. People of all religious persuasions gathered en masse. There were Christians, Jews, Muslims, Unitarians, pantheists, Buddhists, Hindus, Jehovah's Witnesses, Holy Rollers and the Flat Earth Society. They couldn't think of enough ways to say, 'God be with us.'"

"Proceed," God said gently.

"But until then," I said, "and probably still, the church simply isn't what it used to be in America. This, in the same publication, is from Tom Bandy, a United Methodist pastor and author. He said that large numbers of people today believe 'that institutional religion is a sidetrack to spiritual growth, positive mission and world revolution for the good. They see denominations preoccupied by control, politics, ideological and doctrinal agenda that are largely irrelevant to the contemporary situation. They cause more conflicts than they produce peace. They polarize people more than they unite people. They get lost in bureaucracy and hierarchy.'"

I interrupted myself. "God," I said, "do you mind my using what is the mildest of the four letter words?"

"I'll tell you after I hear it."

"What the minister said is a hell of an indictment of organized religion."

"I don't mind that mild four letter word. It IS what you said, or what he said, if (a) all of the churches and other organized places of worship behaved that way and (b) if all of their congregations felt victimized in that way. When you look at the worst sides of organized religion historically, you have to shudder and gag. Millions have been slaughtered in religious wars. Political potentates and thugs acting in the name of God have imposed murderous tyrannies. People have been subjected and enslaved. The list is abominable and almost without end. Disputes in the religious hierarchies have mirrored the worst impulses of humanity—jealousy, arrogance, lust for power and more."

"It sounds hideous."

"It is."

"But why didn't you stop it or guide all these fallible humans into more humane directions. You could have thrown a tantrum, like the great flood of Noah."

"They never did get that story right. There were a lot of floods and there still are, although fewer now that you finally listened to the conservationists and built those big multi-purpose dams."

"God…"

"All right, the point is that I don't go around inflicting these things to punish people. And I don't stop the human corruption and the abuses of religion because what I gave human beings as my greatest gift to them was a free will and choices. I don't know how many times I can say that."

I said, "I believe it."

God seemed relieved.

"So I don't have to tell you that if you find your spiritual search deepened by worshipping in a group, in a place called church, I think that is beautiful and fine. But if you don't get it there, you are free to pursue it elsewhere and in other ways, and I'll find that OK."

"And you are at my side in either place?"

"Do you doubt that?"

"No."

"I told you what saddened me the most was the erosion of faith, because I think everybody needs spiritual health, and the best source for that is a faith or a belief in something. It's needed to put life in some kind of perspective or balance that nourishes both the mind and, if you don't mind my saying it, the soul."

I said I didn't mind. "Some people are troubled by the word 'soul,'" I said, "because they don't really believe in God and they look on 'soul' simply as the spirit within them. That spirit within guides them to thoughts of service and being humane and decent, in other words, shapes their humanity."

"I can't think of a better way to define 'soul,'" God said.

"So why have so many people lost faith, or rather faith in a God?"

"I'd like you to answer that question," God said.

"I think in the early years of belief, faith in a God, or in a lot of gods in the old civilizations, was a way for people to make sense out of life. It gave meaning to a life that was often short and arduous and full of suffering. Their faith was directed toward this mysterious force that they believed would or could control their destiny. Over the centuries people began acquiring knowledge about the world around them. As they became better educated and acquired the freedom to speak and write without fear, they began asking questions that often looked for some evidence of this mysterious power. Blind faith gave way to curiosity and then to doubt and finally rejection of religious faith for large numbers of people. But other millions, like me, searched for a way to rationalize their doubt with their faith."

"And have you succeeded?"

"How can I know? What happened with me is that I simply decided that what appears in much of the Bible is not only allegory but also pure invention written by dubious prophets and political scribes. But some of it—such as the unadorned message of Jesus Christ—is inspiring and powerful and defines in an immortal way what the human being is capable of doing."

"If that was the unadorned message, where did the adornment come in?"

"All the subsequent business of creeds and three-in-one and the virgin birth and the physical ascension. I don't know about that."

"What do you know?"

"I know that while you have materialized here to let me indulge the fancy of a talk with God, I can't truly visualize a God sitting on a Golden Throne dispensing love, passing judgments, communing with angels and being adored. That is still the image of God conveyed in ten thousand Bible studies which also still talk about God's only begotten son…"

"Pardon my intrusion," God said. *"That image stops you. 'God's only begotten son?' Do you think there were more? Less?*

"Well, if you please, God. You tell me. Am I out of line there?"

"What is it about 'only begotten son' that puzzles you?"

"It sounds like a lot of the stories that bloomed in the ages of the mythological gods, the gods who fornicated with mortals, those wild historical myths on which the Greeks have built their tourist industry."

"So how do you read Jesus Christ? Is he something special?"

"Yes."

"Divine?"

"Yes, I think so."

"But not 'God's only begotten son?'"

I had gone too far to retreat now.

"Someone sent by God," I said. "That I can believe. An incarnation of God here on earth."

God was silent.

"Can you help with that?" I asked.

"Yes, but you are a human being. And as you've already candidly reminded me, much of religion is a mystery to you and everybody you know because your mind and their minds are limited. So I couldn't very well tell you what remains a mystery to everybody else."

"But why does it have to be a mystery?"

"Mortal people will be mortal people and God will be God," he said. *"I'm not being mysterious to test people. I'm a creator. I set life in motion. What happens after that is what people do with life. I'm not an official scorer. What happens to you after death is something you must discover. For many people, that fact influences how they conduct their lives. I give love by giving you choices. If I became visible, moved about in some glorified pope-mobile, the mystery is gone out of the relationship between people and God and, if you don't mind, I'll add a small piece of comedy-on-the-square to that."*

"Which is?"

"If all of the mystery about God went up in smoke, the publishing industry would go bankrupt. The Bible would go on 80 per cent discount at all the bookstores. The churches and synagogues and mosques would shut down, and all of those ministers and rabbis and priests and mullahs would have to find work by becoming clinical psychologists and marriage counselors. The world might not recover from all of that mass therapy."

I was about to wince at the prospect of the sudden congestion of marriage counselors, but God interrupted.

"But you're telling me about how your belief has evolved."

"I try hard to get serious about the book of Revelation with its ferocious scenes of earthly convulsion and heaven as some glorious ballroom in the skies. But I can't. If I had to put a label on Revelation I'd call it essentially bunk, although descriptive bunk. Our ideas of God have changed through the centuries because the traits and behavior we attribute to God have changed. The ancients looked on their gods as wrathful and violently punitive if the earthlings got out of line. So we have God in our Bible describing himself as a jealous God who wasn't going to compete with other Gods and he threatened any of the fickle worshippers who put other gods before him.

"Is that what you think, that I am or was, a jealous God?"

"No."

"Why not?"

"Because in those years the designated interpreters of God actually believed you were competing with the earlier wave of gods, so they needed to produce a bylaws of belief which we now know as commandments. In those days, if what we read today is correct, you were the toughest wagonmaster who ever came down the trail, God. Compared with your style, Attila's came right out of the nursery rhymes. You took out towns, wiped out practically all of humanity, and gave Job a really nasty time.

"Do you take all of that literally?"

"No."

"Do you think it happened?"

"No."

"So why do I have a different image today."

"I think it's a lovely thought that man was created in the image of God, although I can think of some horrendous exceptions. But as humanity advanced and learning advanced, we began to understand more about human psychology, about things like our emotional needs, the needs of others, about the beauty of service, vulnerability, what makes human beings human."

"And?"

"I think we've pretty much changed God into the image of man."

"And how has man accomplished that?" he asked.

"I'd say by the attitudes and service we now attribute to God. We call you the God of healing and loving, and benevolent and forgiving. We don't call God judgmental very often these days. I think we've put God through the sensitivity prism that we were exposed to in Basic Counseling and emerged with a God who is Firm but Understanding. He is, therefore, like us when we are at our best. In other words, we might just as well say "Hi, mom" in our new picture of God's most transforming qualities.

"Is that a permanent gender change?"

"No. It's what we've created as a kind of providential unisex."

I paused to apologize. "This has to sound impudent to you," I said. "It's really not intended that way."

God sounded thoughtful. *"I don't hear it that way. In fact, it's close. All right, so you had some form of eclectic belief before this brief encounter, and we can keep exploring. How do you see your God now, and who is your God?"*

"I don't think a belief in God requires the believer, in this case a Christian believer, to accept all of the tales of the Biblical interpretation of God," I said. "Some of those are legends, borrowed from earlier legends. Some of what we call creeds were grafted onto Christianity well after Christ lived for the purpose of tightening the structure of the belief system under assumptions made at the time. The Apostles Creed and The Nicene Creed bind us into solidarity of vow and oath, which is nice. But I really don't know who sitteth at your right hand, God, or if you sitteth at all. I'd like you to answer one question first. The power of God, the part that God once occupied in the centrality of life for most people in this country, has declined. Why is that, would you say?"

"The idea of a God in your lives once meant a universal deity, the creator with powers lasting through time," he said. *"That was the exclusive meaning of God. For many people today, especially people who are in control of their lives and are essentially free, there are gods that have become more important than the one and only and immortal god. They are the gods of gratification and success, of security or status and even the god of freedom itself. Being able to do what you want to do sometimes replaces the*

humility of knowing you are mortal and that eventually you will lose it all. The times they get around to the God we're talking about are the times when those gratifications or living conditions are threatened. In places where lifestyles and attitudes like those are not often available, or available at all, belief is often stronger and so is the expression of belief."

In Islamic countries, for example.

"Yes, there. Belief in many of those countries is structured. Among most Muslims there's a fervor about the expression of belief that is no longer present among most western faiths except for fundamentalists."

Do you approve intensity and fervor in how people express belief?

God considered that.

"Of course. Wouldn't you? I'm not exactly overjoyed when people walk into a church, listen to a chorus of bell-ringers, tolerate the sermon, eat a cookie in the narthex and wrap it up for the week."

"But," I started to say...

"You're right, it's a lot better at least showing up. The trouble with religious intensity is that often it doesn't express the gentler kind of love and humility that becomes true belief. It develops a hard edge, a single minded obsessiveness and sometimes an us-against-them militancy, a 'we're right and everybody else is wrong' attitude."

"Which as we have seen," I said, "can evolve into violence, not only the September 11 kind, but also down through history."

"Yes, where class or ethnic hatred is given a cloak of piety and God is recruited to ennoble murder, war, revenge or greed for power."

"The Islamic terrorists didn't invent that kind of perversion," I said.

"No. It was part of the colonization movement. You also saw it in the European wars of hundreds of years ago, and you still see it when governments aren't wise enough or secure enough to keep religion from getting mixed up in government. Those witch-hunts were an example, but there are a few thousand more. In America, the conviction of some hardcore religionists has led them to want to impose their political agendas on the rest of the country. The resulting turmoil has been pretty ugly. But I don't want to go on this way, because it may sound as though faith as most people understand it is a dying thing. It's not. People are different today than they were hundreds of years ago. They think differently. Most of them think more freely, and a lot of them are finding different ways to sort out and to express their beliefs and to meet their spiritual needs. That doesn't alarm me. Whatever works. So I'm coming back to you. What works for you?"

I said, once more, that I believe. But without being truly irreverent I've tried to remove some of the clutter from my practice of religion.

"I love going to church because I love the communal singing," I said. "I'm touched by the moral I often hear when the sermonizer probes the human spirit and mind, with its kinks as well as its potential for good, and finds a direction that links my own mind and spirit with the teaching of Jesus Christ.

"I know of the recurring theological scrimmages about the historical Jesus Christ, whether Jesus Christ was this or that, whether he was true God as well as man, whether the virgin birth story isn't just another re-weaving of older myths about miraculous births in other cultures. I've explored the possibilities that Jesus Christ isn't all that we learned in childhood. But I also say that in this stage in my life that kind of theological grappling is no longer especially relevant to me. What matters to me about Jesus Christ is that he preached the kind of life that invited us to embrace some simple but profound principles as the heart of spiritual integrity. I translate them this way: a willingness to be open to all who come into our lives and to respect our differences; that we need one another; and that if we can't love everyone in our lives we can at least try to understand; that acknowledging our weakness when we are weak enhances our strength and dignity; that we can search for truth, for ways to serve and for the way of God and still enjoy our humanness. His life, in the imperfect snapshots we have of it, seemed a revelation of God himself. And finally, for me, was the testimony of his death. He was declaring that his truth and his commitment were too precious to renounce. And so he died for them.

"I have to say that for all of their well-documented fumblings, most of the churches I've attended lead me to respect the giving quality of those who sit around me. I appreciate the prod for my own giving that I hear there. I'm stirred when I receive at communion. I'm stirred by all of the symbolism in that act, the history in it, and the intimacy with God that embraces me at that moment, the reconciliation. But church is not necessarily crucial in my belief. I see God's grace in the world around me today, where I didn't years ago. I see God's grace in the clutch of a child's hand, in a public servant's refusal to sacrifice principle in the face of massive pressure and isolation. I feel God's grace when I see two people unbreakably in love with each other.

"I see it on the summit ridge of Kilimanjaro. From there I can look out on the African plain where thousands of men and women were dragged into slavery. And after a few moments I can be brought back to the here and now by a tug on my arm from my African guide, a free man and now a friend. I don't believe that God is installed on a throne in heaven, but I do believe that God is present in the world, in all of it. He is present in all of humanity, the nobility of it and the misery of it. I don't know what God does to direct or manage or alleviate much of the poverty, or if he does any of that. I believe that there is a fundamental goodness in most human beings, and that flows from the spirit of God. And when I see evil in human beings I see that as a misuse or corruption of the power of will with which we are born. I believe God lives within me. If I had to express that spirit in words we use, I'd call it 'conscience.' I know the difference between right and wrong, truth and deceit, generosity and selfishness. God's gift is the power I have to make choices between those directions in conducting my life. Beyond that, I don't really know much about how God actually works."

My conversational partner looked at me enigmatically.

"You have a start," he said.

Chapter 7
Does God choose Americans, Jews, Mormans, Notre Dame?

I described for God a trip I'd made to Egypt a few months after September 11. The country wasn't new to me. In my previous exposures to Egypt I escorted groups of travelers who belong to an adventure travel organization I maintain. Egypt had surprised me. Our experiences there had been some of the most rewarding in my lifetime of travel.

They surprised me because I wasn't thrilled by the prospect of touring Karnak, a temple only slightly smaller than the state of New Jersey. Nor had I piled up huge anticipations about gawking at massive 4.000-year-old statuary that perpetuated the wanton narcissism of the great pharaohs. Walking through interminable corridors of deceased gods with crocodile heads didn't deliver quite the emotional buzz of seeing Everest from the Himalayan fir groves above Namche Bazaar.

And yet I found myself entranced by the vast, numbing loneliness of the desert. I was mesmerized by the Nile, the seminal power of it in shaping the civilizations of the world. I gaped at the supernatural blueness of it against the lifeless desert through which it flowed. Here was the legendary river Nile, an artery of life and hope in the passage of the ages.

It was a place in which to my absolute amazement I found an almost instant sociability among the Egyptians I met. I grant that many of them are promoters, interested in the Yankee dollar or somebody's dollar. They come in regimental strength and they are relentless, peddling plastic mini-pyramids, postcards, camel rides and sacred scarabs of dubious composition. But I also find them to be delightful conversationalists and when they asked me, or us, 'Are you English?' I say, "No, American." And they do a 'Hey, hey, USA, you're okay,' and thumbs up. 'Hi Yo Silver.' Hustlers, sure. But to me at least, the general acceptance of the traveler, an American traveler at that, seemed about the same for Egyptians I'd meet on the street corners and in the cafés. I'm aware the public opinion polls around the world, after Iraq, are likely to challenge these generalizations. I can only share my impressions, and they weren't much different in the winter of 2002 than in the 1990s.

But now I had some thoughts for God that I identified as "worrisome." I told him that what troubled me was something I might call—all right, I did call—super-structured religion that grew out of the historic foundations of organized religion. I said the kind of religious practice I was talking about had the look of robotized worship.

"*Tell me more,*" God said, "*about robotized religion.*"

"How can I tell you," I asked, "without sounding like a hypocrite?"

God seemed amused. *"We keep haggling over that word. Why should you be immune to hypocrisy?"*

He seemed pleased with himself for asking the question. I felt relieved. God might be tougher on Judgment Day, if he ever really declared one, but he was cream and marshmallows today.

"I thought hypocrisy was a rather universal character trait," he said. *"Relax. You're just one of the boys."*

"You have a marvelous way with words," I congratulated God. He sat back, inviting me to expound.

I told of once more hearing the call to prayers over the loudspeakers and from the mosques from Cairo to Luxor to Aswan. I said I understood the genuine devotion of the Muslims who observed the call and bent to the East. I said it was impressive.

"So far," God said, *"it doesn't sound very objectionable to me."*

"Not objectionable at all," I said. "When I was a kid attending the Roman Catholic mass, one of the priest's assistants or servers would ring a little bell and we'd all kneel and tap our chests and say, 'through my fault, through my fault, through my most grievous fault.' We'd do that three times, while the priest would raise the communion wafer he was consecrating, and then we would all file toward the altar to receive communion."

"Yes," God said, *"that is another ritual with which I'm familiar. And by the way, I want you to know that I find that as acceptable as the other one you talked about."*

"God," I said, "Give me some room. I'm trying to make a point."

"Which is?"

"I first want to affirm this: I have great respect for the good that much of organized religion performs in the ailing world. Its generosity has saved millions of lives and bettered the lives of millions of others, once we're past the stage when evangelistic religion acted as a willing arm of political adventurers and colonizing potentates and powers. Church is OK with me. I enjoy worshipping as part of a community and I'm stirred by it. I'm brought to tears by the sound and lyrics of some of the old hymns we sing together."

"Such as?" God asked.

"Well, a hymn like 'Spirit of God,' when we sing 'stoop to my weakness, strength to me impart…'"

"And what moves you about those words?"

"They create a picture for me of a God of great power but also humility—or if a powerful God can't quite be humble, then compassion—who would kneel beside me to comfort me."

There was no sound in the room for a few moments. God then spoke quietly. *"That's a lovely thought,"* he said.

"Does it make sense?"

Another pause.

"Why or how could I argue with what you've just said? Why would I? But now I have to know about this robotized religion that's troubling you."

I entered that terrain uneasily, conflicted and mired immediately in a dilemma, trying to resolve my thoughts. Communal worship was important to me. Being part of a processional of belief reaching back more than 2,000 years comforted me and humbled me in wonder and thanksgiving. I felt tugs of sentiment in the echoes of those long ago bells summoning me to bow my head in the children's service in my hometown. And I conceded that membership in that community demanded or at least required an acceptance of some or all of its dogma. And there in Egypt I was aware of multitudes prostrating themselves obediently, and unequivocally at the high-pitched cries of the muezzin.

"I know it's unfair," I said, "and I'm part of the same automated ritual in my faith. But there's another and unsettling side to some of those rituals."

God seemed genuinely engrossed in the mystery of where I was going.

"One of the sticking points for me is what feels like a mandate to accept the mythology of the organized faith—its "sacred" canons or books—to qualify for membership in the lodge. It comes down to a feeling of indoctrination, the recital of creeds in the Christian church, for example, that are founded on somebody's vision or surmise or fantasy, years after Christ. There are scenes on television of Islamic children reading fervently from a book, making body movements in unison, growing up in an orchestrated, regimented expression of solidarity. Those scenes are scary. You see there the beginnings of an us-against-them cadre of the future."

God's gaze seemed to wander, as though picking its way through thistles of tangled politics and theology, and the unease of the penitent in front of him.

"How do YOU want to worship God?" he asked.

"I'd like to feel free to take some of the mythology with which I grew up and separate it from faith. I want to believe in a universal spirit of God, transcending life but nurturing and animating my life, opening a road to a moral and generous life if I wish to choose it."

"Do you think all people want to worship in that way?" God asked.

"No. I think millions of people—Christians, Muslims, Jews and others—are comfortable wrapped in a full acceptance of the traditional creeds and dogma of their religion. And they might look on me as vacillating and an opportunist. Worse, an agnostic."

God wrinkled his forehead in some dissatisfaction.

"Ah, that word again. Agnostics don't bother me much, I have to tell you. Most people wonder about

the faith in which they worship, if they have one. That's more true than ever now that you have a thousand TV channels spewing news, sitcoms, war, ball games, and information—information, mother lodes of information. And I don't have to tell you the search for peace for millions of people who don't quite know its source does not go simply from a Sunday morning service to a quiet brook. I know that huge numbers of those people don't look on the Sunday morning service, or Saturday service, or Friday prayers, as the watershed of that peace. A lot of them shun organized worship as constricting and arid. So where else? The therapist's office? Well, that's where it is for some of them. Meditationals? Yes. And then there is the benediction some feel they receive in nature, deepened by nature's total absence of judgment. Yes, that. AA meetings? Sure. Millions get it there. Their God may be the conventional God. Or if they can't quite bring themselves to accept this benevolent and forgiving Super Being, because he carries all this baggage of dogma and ritual, they WILL accept calling it Higher Power. It is a strength somewhere that supports them and answers their need for a sheltering goodness without which they cannot fight off addiction. That need is powerful. Their belief that there is a nuturing strength beyond them is powerful."

"I have such a need," I said, "and such a belief."

"Yet this is where the agnostic leaves you. You believe now, after all of your wanderings and your probing, in the God of your childhood."

"I believe in the God of my childhood but I don't believe in all of those visitations of God on earth that are relentlessly proclaimed in the holy books. I don't believe in the acts of tumult, tempest and retaliation attributed to God, or the rearrangement of the earth's geography because God was feeling owly about public behavior. I don't believe there are chosen people of God. I don't believe God chose the Mormons, Jews, the Maasai in Africa, the Americans, the Muslims or anybody else who makes the claim based on a supernatural experience or Gallup Polls. I especially don't believe the favored ones who say *their* supernatural experience is documented, verifiable and beyond all attempts at refutation and, all other claims are dissed as pipe dreams."

God interrupted.

"You say you try to follow the preachments of Jesus Christ."

"I try imperfectly, of course."

"But Christianity is a direct and lineal descendent of Judaism. Christ was a Jew and the Christian Church organically couples its New Testament with the Jewish Bible and accepts the Old Testament as reverently as it does the New. And the Old Testament is unmistakable in professing that God made Jews his chosen people. Now I have to ask you. If you don't believe God singled out a people as the chosen one—and I'm not saying I did—then aren't you stuck in a place of logic that de-Christianizes you?"

"God," I said, "I know you would never lower yourself to trick questions."

"You're right," he said. *"I don't ask questions that would incriminate the questionee."*

"We're agreed, and thank you for that assurance."

"So will you answer the question?"

"Is the question: have I abdicated as a Christian because I don't believe God singled out a people for his special blessing and guidance?"

"It is the question."

"My answer is that I certainly don't believe God ordained any one people as his preferred. I don't believe he acts through one preferred people. And I don't believe he ordered the destruction of Jericho, either. I'm aware that Jesus Christ preached from the Old Testament, but not exclusively from the Old Testament. But it's his summons to service and equality and love and generosity that draws me, not his scriptural citations or how or where he was born or what happened in the tomb. I believe the Bible embodies a priceless guide to life for a person of God but I don't believe some of its fantasies or some of its history and political ax-grinding. Not accepting those doesn't mean, for me, that I've cashiered myself as a Christian, although I admit I probably wouldn't get elected Pope. I probably wouldn't get elected chairman of the Lutheran potluck committee, either, but I know people who would and I am glad to worship with them."

"Why do you feel so comfortable with that position?

"Well, I think you said it yourself, God. You were noncommittal about whether you've chosen a certain people or not."

"That doesn't mean I haven't."

"No. But it doesn't mean you have. And I understand you have this intuitive and practical need to be mysterious."

"The fact that you can't comprehend the way of God doesn't mean I have some scheme to keep you ignorant about it. I've told you before: If I answered all of these questions we'd either empty all of the churches and synagogues and mosques in the world or wreck all of them by starting a stampede to get in. I'm trying to give you some guidance and comfort. I don't want to turn you into another prophet. You don't have that propheteering charisma.

"No. I did come to you with these dilemmas. How much of the conventional teaching can I question before I find myself persona non grata."

"To whom?

"To you."

"Do you see yourself in danger of that?"

"No."

"Then what is the problem?"

It was a reasonable question. What WAS the problem?

I hesitated longer than I wanted to. I wanted to think this through but I didn't want to throw the whole cart upside down and let doubts about some of those mythologies spill into disarray. I'd been through that. I believed. But I was also mystified, and there was beauty in some of that mystery and—

God was generous.

"Let's go past the horror of religious groups acting in God's name and spilling blood in their arrogance and insanity. Those things have happened for thousands of years and they're happening today. The rewards of avowing a faith in community, such as church, synagogue or mosque, are clear to me and have brought comfort and nurture to billions of people over the centuries. Now let me ask you a question. Never mind what the attitudes of religious institutions were centuries ago or generations ago. Never mind that in some of those religious institutions today a rigid conformity is demanded, and if it isn't performed, the result is ostracism or even death. Some people have really not learned. But where you worship today, do you feel such a demand for conformity? Let's say you doubt the story, do you think they would drum you out of the church you attend?"

Before answering I asked God to clarify his question. "You're not insisting that dialogue, with Job, actually happened."

"My lips," God said, *"are sealed."*

I thought that was a reasonable answer. And I said, "No, the church I attend, and most of the ones like it that I'm aware of, wouldn't in the 21st Century insist on that kind of orthodoxy to stay in the church."

"And so to conclude," God said: *"You believe, but in the church in which you worship there are tenets and scriptural trappings that just aren't part of your belief system. God is in your life but you don't think you have to sign off on all of the legends and the begats and the golden trumpetry."*

"Yes."

"Are you at ease with your belief? Does it ask for humility in the presence of something you believe is good but can't fully understand? And do you accept that humility and give your trust and love in return?"

"Yes."

"If you are at ease with that," God said, *"so am I."*

"But," he added, *"try to do it better."*

Chapter 8
Imagine a ball game in the sky

When sports zealots gather around a few grogs, there's always a threat that somebody is going to construct a ball game in the sky. And we'll get a picture of the ultimate battle in the Eternity League: Babe Ruth at the plate and Cy Young on the mound.

I asked God if he had ever seen or scheduled such an epic contest.

"Sooner or later in this business you see everything," God acknowledged. *"But that's one that I've missed. Are you sure both of those guys got into this place?"*

"If you mean heaven, God, I'm not sure that we've arrived at a conclusion about heaven. Some visionaries portray it as a sort of gold-plated convention center for card-holding saints who are so credible that nobody ever asks to see their IDs, which is heavenly enough. Others say it's really a lush aviary of disembodied spirits who float in peace forever and communicate subliminally."

God emitted what I would have sworn was a grunt. *"Neither one sounds all that irresistible to me,"* he said.

"But you know what the afterlife is all about, and you're not saying," I nagged.

"I do know and I have to assure you it's a lot better than what was described to you. I don't have to give you all of the ground rules. You're still trying to qualify. But I will tell you I haven't seen Babe Ruth yet and you might say it's getting late."

"Maybe he can get in under the veterans-in-waiting category," I said. "I'm curious about one other guy, God. I knew a football character named Johnny Blood. His real name was John McNally. He came from a well-to-do family with a background in publishing. He was a handsome rogue who played professional football for Green Bay and Pittsburgh, and at an early date developed a thirst for martinis and a hankering for blondes. He missed curfew all the time and once escaped detection from a shady, off-limits hotel parlor in the 1930s by hanging by his fingernails from the ledge of an eighth story window. He had an extraordinary mind and later taught college mathematics and economics. But his academic passion was poetry. In his later years, on nights before the National Football League championship games, I'd see him holding a poetry recital, weaving unevenly under the hot air register, speaking beautifully to a make-believe audience..."

God interrupted, *"Reciting Hamlet's soliloquy from Shakespeare, never missing a syllable, standing under a fake fern?"*

"That's the guy," I said. "I was one of the writers who voted him into the Hall of Fame at Canton."

"Well, he must have taken the wrong turn to Canton because he ended up here." God said. *"Wavy white hair kind of guy, every strand in place, strong, ruddy features, soft confidential voice, pleasant and quietly persuasive, sounding like a veteran Shakespearean who might have acted with Barrymore?"*

"Yeah," I said. "That's Johnny Blood. How did he get in there?"

"I understand he talked his way in. And once he got in everybody sort of adopted him and figured him to be right out of the repertory of Old Vic. You say he played football?

"A halfback and punter," I said. "Old timers said he once jumped off a team train on the way to a game because he couldn't pay a gambling debt."

"Did he get hurt?"

"No. He picked a river crossing because he was a great swimmer. He jumped because the guy to whom he owed the money was a 250-pound tackle who hated halfbacks. Have you got many 250-pound tackles around there?"

"They seldom show."

"Give my regards to John the next time you see him."

"I doubt that I can. When he gets going on Hamlet he hates to be interrupted."

"By the way, now that you described John, how do people show up in the afterlife if there is something tangible about them. Is it how they looked when they took their last breath, or when they were in their prime? Do they get an option on that?"

"My son," he said. *"I'm really not thrilled being grilled this way. We still haven't addressed what constitutes the afterlife venue and, between you and me, we're not going to. I want you to have incentives. Pick your venue and go for it."*

"It must be a trial being God," I mumbled.

"It is," he said. *"It's a trial when I'm invoked by the people you're talking about, the athletes and the coaches and the fans. Look. I don't really want to talk about it. You can't believe the things they ask for."*

"I can," I said. "On my high school basketball team, we used to pray to go to the state tournament."

"Did you get there?"

"Yes."

"What happened?"

"We lost by 35 points."

God looked off, seemingly disappointed to hear the news. *"Be careful.."* he started to say...

"What you pray for?" I asked.

"Yes, well, you know the axiom. My notes tell me you used to be involved in athletics off and on."

"Yes. I wrote about professional football and other games from time to time for newspapers and in books. It came up once in a while, all of the petitions athletes make to God. Practically everybody does that as part of their prayers, the kitchen sink list. But the ones that must be particularly tiresome are the ones coming from the jocks—I'm sorry God. I slipped into the locker room vernacular there."

"Well, I've heard worse. I don't think tiresome is the word I'd use. I mean tending to the lives of people is what I'm about. Prayer is the people's expression of their vulnerability, their hopes and their thanksgiving. Sometimes prayer is the mark of their commitment and sometimes it just means they're scared spitless, if you don't mind the vernacular. You're right about one thing. I've heard it all. Not long ago a forward on the West Bend hockey team in one of the American towns prayed very earnestly about wanting to score a goal that night to set the league record. He was very polite and humble. He said if it was my will for him to score a goal, he would be very thankful."

I said I liked the young forward's approach to prayer.

"Yes. By coincidence, the goalie for the East Bend team offered a prayer the same day. He said he would very much like to score a shutout in the game because not only would his team probably

win if he did, but he would set a league record for shutouts in a season."

"And he, too, was polite?"

"Extremely. He said it was against his religious upbringing to turn all of his prayers into a plea for favors. But this was very important to him and he humbly asked for the strength to make it happen."

"What a quandary, God," I said. "What did you do?"

"I turned it over."

I was startled. God is turning it over? "To whom did you turn it over, God?"

God receded for a moment into a kind of providential ambivalence.

"I turned it over to the referee. I mean, I let the game go on and let the players' abilities and efforts decide it, which I think was the fairest way to do it."

"Then what you're saying, God, is that the prayers, or at least the prayers of one of the players, were wishful thinking."

"That is NOT what I'm saying. We're not going to return to the question of why some prayers are answered and others not. Or, in fact, if ANY prayers are answered in terms of a direct intervention by God. You have scholars who use a word I'm going to use. For mortals, that has to remain an imponderable. Millions of people believe their prayers have in

fact been answered. I'm not going to tell you they aren't. The relationship between people and God is one that must remain an essential matter of faith. That faith doesn't go only to a belief or wish to live happily ever after in heaven or in some environment of reward. It also influences how they conduct their lives and shapes their value. The sight of a kid praying for a shutout in hockey is not going to offend the kid's God. Why should it? In praying for an outcome that brings honor and praise to him the kid is pretty much a normal human being. But the simple act of prayer, of sharing his fragileness and baring his vanity and asking for fulfillment matters. Asking for the companionship of someone or something higher in his quest makes the kid better and deeper and larger. He could have asked simply to be given the strength to play as well as he could possibly play. I suppose that might be a less self-serving prayer, but if I'm not going to quibble about that, why should his spiritual advisors?"

"It makes sense," I said.

"I think so. Now whether the boy's prayers were actually answered is something the theologians can argue. The act of prayer, simply praying and being honest about it, is the true core of the beauty of that moment of unity. It joins the human—the sinner who is a penitent—to his or her God. One of the loveliest words in your language, and one of the loveliest expressions of a spiritual presence in human lives, is the belief in the grace of God. When you accept that there is such a thing, you have penetrated to the heart of the value of prayer. Some

people pray to accept God's will, which brings a nourishment of its own, the realization that there is so much in humans' lives that is beyond their control. Psychologists might have an explanation there, but why should that be any conflict between the advocates of clinical psychology and those who seek a healthy relationship between God and humans? Psychologists probe the mysteries of the mind and try to foster or restore emotional health. God, well, cleans up after the mess. People look at changes in their lives, both the good and painful changes in their lives, and call that God's will. If it comforts them to believe that, then they have received one of the true blessings of prayer. They feel healed or reconciled in acceptance. What constitutes the true will of God I'm going to leave to your theologians. We started this by looking at that special relationship between athletes and God. I say special because athletes are so visible in the world today on television, and that's not only the world class athletes but athletes of any description. One thing I noticed in the last 20 or 30 years or so was what I'd call the "Hey, thank you God" celebration that so many of the athletes put on after scoring. There was one especially who couldn't restrain his exuberance and his gratitude and he'd point to the sky as though God was calling signals."

"Cris Carter, who played the Minnesota Vikings," I said.

"Do you have an opinion?" God asked.

"I do. To begin with, Carter is a devout man who has not been immune to acts of selfishness on the field, judgmental outbursts directed at teammates and harangues intended to boost his own goals. He is a devout man today in response to his recovery from an ugly time in his life when he was both selfish and chemically addicted. He has also been a great athlete. His celebration of his discipleship in the middle of the game was genuine.

"I know that now. When I first saw it I was on the brink of retching. It struck me as a pretty gross form of grandstanding: 'Hey, I'm a believer. I want the world to know that. I'm giving God the credit for the touchdown.' My attitudes on athletes publicly bringing religion into the ballpark reach back 30 years to when I wrote often about ballplayers and their games, and I've recycled those attitudes several times. I first was impressed with star athletes holding chapel services in a hotel room a few hours before a ball game. Theirs was a private worship, in which they renewed their faith and asked to be allowed to play at the limit of their strength, and that no one be injured on either side. These were celebrated athletes bowing in humility, acknowledging that there were values in their lives that came before winning.

"And yet when I went into the locker room after the game to interview some of these same athletes, I would react in the way of most of my colleagues when a player invoked God or Jesus Christ as the source of the team's victory or his touchdown catch. What the player recited into the tape recorder was a passionate tribute to the glory of God for his fingernail catch in the end zone with two defenders hanging on his shoulder pads and belt buckle. Inwardly I grimaced when I'd hear that kind of testimonial. A quotation like that almost always let the air out of the story because it pulled the reader out of the action and conflict of the ballpark and plopped him into a Sunday school.

"So most of those quotes didn't get into the newspaper. Usually the rest of the player's post-game remarks did. Years later—and I have to say it was after I'd experienced a trauma in my personal life and returned to God—I realized how truly arrogant I had been about that, inflicting a gratuitous censorship on the athlete. If the player had made some kind of off-color comment that still fell within the guidelines of acceptable blue, I'd probably have written it. When he talked about God's presence in the huddle, I often didn't. That was more culpable than arbitrary censorship. It was a misuse of the right of selectivity that is implicit in the reporting trade. I thought a player bringing God into the locker room was some kind of half-baked evangelism that didn't belong in a newspaper story. I thought that through over the years. My first impulses were wrong. If the player wants to credit God, he has the right to do that and you have the responsibility to give him that courtesy if he happened to be a player involved in an important part of the game. If he weren't, you probably wouldn't be interviewing him in the first place. You don't have to give him 15 column inches to deliver his witness. But you shouldn't ignore it, either."

"And that is how you feel today?"

"Yes. Not militantly, but I have changed the way I feel about it. About the demonstration of the Cris Carters, I can handle those in moderation. I can also handle players kneeling in the end zone to give thanks, as long as they don't try to lead the congregation, the crowd, in 'A Mighty Fortress is Our God.'"

"You're still a little spiky on that, my dear fellow," God said.

"Well, a little. And it might be because I think that people who live visible lives have an unusual forum to express themselves, and sometimes that forum is grossly abused for personal advantage when it touches on religion. But whether those glory-to-God statements are religiously oriented or simply meant to attract attention, I dislike most demonstrations of any kind at the ballpark. When I started writing about football the guy ran 70 yards, turned and handed the ball to the official. I grant that we live in another time of athletic self-expression. I am coping, God."

But give me your own thoughts, I was about to ask.

"Yes, I'll give you my thoughts briefly. I would be the last to tell you that God is bothered by hearing a tasteful commercial here and there with 70 million people watching on television. I agree with some of your objections to excessive demonstration of piety. About those references to 'the help of God' and 'God willing' and 'praise God' and the rest. People, of course, do that all the time. And I find it becoming and a truly central part of their lives, the idea that God is near. I like the expression of humility that

whatever gains have come to them weren't totally a product of their genius or artistry or work. Something higher deserves some of the credit. Now this may or may not be true. We will let the theologians argue that, too. But a person's willingness to share the credit with some benevolent spirit is something that goes very deeply to that person's civility and actual faith. When it is insincere or calculated, of course, there isn't enough contempt to characterize that kind of duplicity. What I'm saying is this: People seem content to allow politicians plenty of slack in tossing around the name of God. It suggests in a lot of cases that "We're God's people." Well, I wouldn't want to see them try to prove that. And all of those references to "a nation under God" are a little redundant, in my judgment. The United States of America is a nation under God. For sure. So are Indonesia, Zimbabwe and Monte Carlo. God couldn't very well be a god for one nation and not another.

"So what this tells you is that when I hear an athlete go into a litany to thank God for his spectacular catch, I have no reason to doubt his or her sincerity. Writers can quote them or not, or they can get tired of the liturgy. But if the guy wants to express himself as a spiritual person in the context of his game, why shouldn't he be granted respect?"

I said I could think of no reason.

"Then," God said, *"we are in harmony and agreement."*

I don't know what took us so long.

Chapter 9
All right, God; do you program our lives?

I slipped a yellow legal notepad out of my briefcase and drew a look of mild apprehension from God.

He stood and glanced at his watch. We had no rigid parameters of time in this interview but I gathered we were approaching the end. He didn't seem impatient but the suggestion seemed relatively clear.

His watch fascinated me. On the face of it glowed 12 tiny lightning bolts. "Do those little flashes of lightning denote the hour?" I asked.

"Uhh, no."

What then?

"Each one represents a millennium," God said.

"And you change watches every…" I began.

"12,000 years," he said.

Nice, I thought. It explained why God did not seem to be in any special hurry to end the conversation.

But he remained standing comfortably by the window and inquired about the notepad.

"On this I've jotted some of the most pressing questions volunteered to me by a friend who took a random sampling of her own friends. The questions dealt with their mystification about the ways of God. What would you ask God if you had the chance?"

God sat down to assay the weight of this line of discussion.

"It sounds a little like an arraignment," God said.

"I think it's just people wanting clarity," I said.

"And they don't think they achieve clarity in the sermons they hear?" God asked mischievously.

"Er, well, they might call clarity in their sermons an oxymoron."

"And why is that?"

"Partly, I suppose, because the good preachers have to lean on the Scriptures and sometimes, often, the Scriptures are ambiguous or plainly fanciful."

"I'd like to hear some of the questions."

I lifted the introductory page and read from my friend's ledger:

> **Why doesn't God offer a cure for some diseases like Alzheimer's?**

> Why does he permit a sick person to suffer so much pain before dying?
>
> Why did he allow six million Jews to be killed?
>
> Why does he permit some of his servants, such as priests and ministers, to disobey their vows and basic senses to abuse children and others?

God held up his hand unobtrusively and momentarily seemed to drift in thought. He nodded his head. *"In court, they hold an arraignment after they bring an indictment. What you have from your friend on that notepad are questions, I grant that. But they also sound very much like a prosecution. I know they're not intended to be that. Millions of people who believe or want to believe in a God of mercy and fairness and understanding cannot comprehend why this God would 'allow' those terrible events and those betrayals and suffering. They try to comprehend but don't have answers. And many of them get angry with God. Most of these people also believe in a God of limitless power. They remember the stories in the Bible about the seas parting and other miracles—whether or not those events actually happened—and then they ask, 'Why wouldn't the same God intervene to save lives or to prevent pain?'"*

"That," I said, "about sums it up. I think we've been through this before, but these are very specific pains and, if I might say it, these are what seem to be some serious hostility directed at God's sense of justice.

"You have some additional questions on that pad," God said.

I continued with my friend's list.

> How do we know that God is our savior?
>
> Why does God permit one religion to fight and kill others strictly because they have a different religion?
>
> If there is only one God, why do some people kill and maim in his name?"
>
> Why do some ministers of God, who have sworn allegiance to God, steal from their churches and temples?
>
> Does God have anything to do with the "near death" experiences that have been reported?
>
> There is a Bible, Torah, Koran and others. Which is the 'real' book of God? Is there only one God and, if so, why does he exist under so many different names to the various sects describing him as "their" God and therefore the one and only.

"And this is the final question," I said:

> What is the connection between God and a soul?

I had an irrational impulse to picture God as a defendant. I hurriedly snuffed out that notion but was relieved to see no aggrieved look from God after he'd listened to these crusty depositions. He did say:

"Maybe I should put in a call to Johnny Cochran."

"I don't seen any TV cameras," I said. "Johnny may not show."

"There's a bedrock assumption in most of those questions," God said. *"Most people of faith—and puzzlement—ask them in one form or other. I don't blame them. Their assumption is that if God is omnipotent and can control all he surveys, then why doesn't he prevent evil or suffering."*

"It IS a somewhat logical question," I said. "First, the omnipotent part. Are you omnipotent?"

God measured his response. Mortals, after all, are not famous for examining all shadings and nuances when they ask a question like that.

"If there is one true God of all people," he said. *"the creator and the source of good and love, then God must be, MUST be, all-powerful."*

There didn't appear to be a whole lot of nuances in that answer.

I needed to acknowledge that. "No matter how you cut it," I said, "there is nothing divisible or arguable about that."

"No, there isn't."

"But there is evil in the world."

"There is evil and hunger and suffering and pain and sorrow and unfairness and death," God acknowledged.

The room went silent. The air density added pounds of pressure. I have to say I wasn't sure whether God was going to disappear right there, or I was going to disappear, or some dreadful drumroll was going to announce the presence of the Prince of the Netherworld, tails, horns, Gounod's music and all.

None of that happened.

"There is also generosity and sacrifice and beauty and love and friendship and forgiveness," God said.

"And those clashing forces coexist in humanity," I observed.

"They do. Humanity was created by God. Human beings are fallible and mortal. They can produce marvelous works and ideas and breathe love and beauty into much of what they do. Human beings are also capable of hatred, and greed, and hunger for power. They can enslave other people or ennoble them, slaughter or heal, all these things. Throughout history the perversions of human nature—those parts susceptible to delusion, to turning resentment and frustration into hatred, to revenge and to the gratifications of power—have led to genocide, torture, political oppression and the impoverishment of whole peoples."

"And yet in most or all of these cases, doesn't an all-powerful God have a choice of intervening to stop it?"

"An all-powerful God could intervene. But if the whole thrust of his creation is to allow the interaction of the humanity he's brought to life, then he will not take on the role of some super-orchestrator and arrange endgame scenarios."

That was a proposition to ponder: a God who was hands-off, with exceptions I'm sure he'd acknowledge, once he has created the divine spark of life. 'That's a concept, a passive God, that a lot of people would have trouble accepting," I said.

"The word 'passive' God is yours. It's inappropriate and it's wrong. But adopting my language—If you don't mind—do you have any trouble accepting a God who does not intervene in the flow of human history, politically, medically or geologically, but does ENTER human lives powerfully and decisively?"

I said I accepted that equation as the way of God. "I know that preachers and theologians have to resist part of it because while they affirm the creed of salvation by faith and grace, things happen in our lives and the lives of nations that are crying to be explained and just can't be explained theologically. It's an awkward place for oracles in the pulpit. Their refuge—and this is not easy—is to suggest that these things are either God's will, which surpasses all understanding, or they happen for reasons that have to remain a mystery. Almost all of us console ourselves with one truth about the way of God, that there is so much we don't and cannot understand. But I have to follow my own belief in this, and I don't think God tries to control our lives or the earth, or that he lays out a specific agenda for each individual. I believe this explains why catastrophes occur, why wars occur, why people kill each other and rob from each other and why millions are treated unfairly by life; why people lie as well as admit being wrong; why people sin as well as love, give as well as act selfishly. I hope you will not consider this an insolent question, but if that is largely true, and God lets people be people, what DOES God do?"

"I didn't say God is idle. It was you who implied that, although you did it with due deference. We've talked about the most intimate connection people have with God, which is prayer. Most people believe that at one time or another their prayers have been answered. And they're right. The outcome they prayed for may or may not have been exactly what they sought. But there WAS an outcome that eased their pain or stress. These aren't word games. The human heart and mind are capable of wonders, but they are also fragile. What they crave most is peace. The one to whom they pray is mindful of that and understands, and can lead that person to peace. Have you experienced that?"

"I have."

"Have you experienced moments of despair so deep as to be unbearable, or anguish because of a loss in your life or because of your behavior? And did these periods make you so distraught that you found yourself helpless and isolated? And, in this worst imaginable grief, you have asked God for help?"

"I have."

"And did you feel comforted?"

"I did."

"What else did you feel?"

"I felt the presence of God. I felt cleansed."

"And why do you think that was?"

"I admitted my helplessness. I admitted my deceptions and the injuries I had inflicted on those who depended on me and loved me."

God asked if I minded an evaluation of where our conversation had carried us in the last 15 minutes.

"I'm the last guy to claim immunity," I said.

"In your mind God is not a pro-active mastermind influencing the course of world events, allowing some things to happen, defusing others. Some terrible things happen, in other words, on 'God's watch,' to quote the political jargon. On the other hand you agree that each individual who is open to God's presence and benevolence can experience that."

"A God," I said, "who is also there for our admission of wrong, and for our plea for forgiveness."

"That, too. And how would you reconcile this with your opinion that while God has the power to heal and comfort, this power does not always answer a prayer to spare a life that is failing?"

"Humans are mortal," I said. "If all prayers to spare

a life were answered, nobody would die. I think one can believe in a loving and generous God without requiring him to repeal the laws of pathology."

God put his hands together the way a sociologist would to introduce a summation.

"I'm hardly a passive God. I'm an indwelling God. You asked about God and the soul. The 'soul' is one of those subjective words whose meaning can be argued. I'd call 'soul' the spirit of God imbued in each human being. That is the gift of God. At one time or other, in one form or other, most humans have the gift of choice. They can choose this act or that act, this road or that. It may not seem possible that even the poorest of the poor have choices, but somewhere most of them do. This isn't saying that they all have equal opportunity. Far from that. God created the earth. But what happens on earth is in the hands of the people who live on it and in the laws of nature that God has set in motion.

"The power that God does exert is to heal and nourish and comfort, to touch each heart with the possibility of love and goodness. Every person who reaches maturity, who has the choice of acting on what he or she knows to be right or wrong, good or bad, generous or selfish, has been born with a will to act on those instincts."

"That is what God offers you, a gift that can bless your spirit, your life and the lives of those around you, if you wish that."

I told God all outstanding indictments had disappeared.

Chapter 10
The pilgrim grapples with how he prays

God exhaled airily. He seemed good-natured in a mixed attitude of satisfaction and bemusement. He got up from his chair in his casual clothes and stepped closer for some farewell thoughts.

He was smiling as though dabbling with a secret, but he didn't give the appearance of being the God of condescension. So I wondered what he had in mind. I surveyed the terrain. Maybe I should brace for a sermon from the father of all sermons. I had a horrific thought. Can you imagine God himself, from a pulpit, putting the wood to sweating parishioners for their tightwad donations to the building fund?

Maybe he wanted to hear my confession: "Father forgive me for being, what? A theological klutz? Impulsive?" Or, he might offer a benediction. Wouldn't that bring down the curtain? When was the last time I'd heard it in real time, *Dominus Vobiscum?* But here he was, signing off and now being affable and relaxed about it, almost bustling around, like the neighborhood pharmacist ending the day. Then he squared up and confronted me, and I couldn't see how I was going to avoid some kind of judgment.

He'd obviously scanned my mind. *No,"* he said, *"I'm not throwing the book at you. This is an interview, not a prosecution. I do want to know what you think now. Do you know more about me or more about yourself?"*

I said I hadn't expected him to reveal the secrets of the universe. I already believed in a power greater than myself, to quote an expression popular among people, including me, who have had to remove alcohol from their lives. What I'd been looking for, I said, was something that would—

"That would more or less confirm your own suppositions about God and how God moves in the world. Isn't that about it?"

"We don't have many secrets, do we," I said.

"Hardly any."

"As for me," I said, "life until my later years came down to the need for some kind of fulfillment I could define. The center of my life for years was gratification. There's no point in trying to disguise it to myself and certainly not to you. You could subdivide that by emotional gratification and by physical gratification. In other words, by achieving something."

"How did you do that?"

"By work, by professional achievement, by physical exertion toward some goal. I was a newspaperman, a communicator. I wrote stories, opinion columns, profiles of people famous and obscure, people we defined as ordinary but who lived extraordinary lives. Sometimes I wrote simply to entertain, to tell a good story. Somebody said I was a minstrel. I gave speeches and wrote books and conducted radio and television shows. In my community I was relatively visible and reasonably respected. On some days I could make a positive difference in the lives of some who read my column. I could redress a social abuse. That was gratifying. I was an adventurer. I climbed mountains and bicycled and skied in the wilderness. That, too, was gratifying. I had two daughters to whom I should have extended more intimate love. But I was busy. Selfish, I suppose."

"You suppose?"

"I was selfish. I had endless reserves of energy for work and exploring the world and for life, and in the midst of this I served my community in a way that I thought met my obligations professionally and personally. But I neglected those who were closest to me. I discovered that later."

"Did you say 'discovered?'

God took apart my sophistry with easy and soundless strokes, like a disinterested surgeon removing an appendix.

I corrected myself. "I didn't discover it. I admitted it, to myself and to them. I made apologies, and for a while I hated the imposter I'd been. I got myself together later in life, in ways that restored my connection with God, with you."

"What were you seeking before you changed direction?"

"Living to the max, finding self-satisfaction by doing everything in overdrive, by performing and risking, even by rehabilitating in overdrive. I got fat covering a pro football team and I took off 55 pounds in four months. I changed dimensions so fast they began referring to me in the past tense in the office."

"In your mind did all that exertion and achieving make your life successful?"

"It made life thrilling."

"As you know, that wasn't the question."

I was aware of that. I said I had a built a life on powering into each day and filling it. I know that sounds melodramatic, and it probably was.

"Most people," God said, *"are self-absorbed in some way. This is their life, their world. What they derive from life is important. Of course it is. Most people are able to achieve a balance in how they commit their energies and resources and emotions. I'm not sure you did, at least until later. No matter what station a person occupies in life there has to be a place in it for genuine love, for lifting yourself out of yourself. This means caring for others, nourishing them, and carrying their loads if they need. I hope you believe there's been love in yours. Everybody sins and almost everybody is guilty of selfishness in some form, trying to drain what they can out of their skills and ambition. You were self-absorbed but you also performed some service, so you were, well, human. Don't chop yourself up too strenuously. By the way, how long did it take you to learn how to extend love?"*

"About the time," I said, "that it took me to reduce my self-deceptions."

"Was it that much of a project?"

"It was," I said. "It took all those years of self-indulgence before I could figure you out."

"To figure out God? Well, that is a novel way to describe what most people call search. And what was your conclusion?"

"I used those words, God, to put a knock on my head. It took me awhile to discover that the world wasn't invented to be my sandbox. First I have to say that there are limits to the virtues of most people I know and certainly there've been to mine. No matter how much we try to recognize and wring out our darker qualities, we are sometimes prone to greed, resentment, selfishness and stupidity."

"That's a pretty impressive load in four words."

"There are sequels, as you know. What I mean is that we are highly imperfect and often unfair. To be blunt, sometimes we're absolute louts. This is hardly a secret either to school principals, police sergeants or God. And now I'll stop saying 'we' and change the pronoun. I was the guy nursing most of those unsanitary attitudes and some of that behavior. And then when I learned something about humility, I asked myself what God would see as an acceptably good life for me. I concluded that what God wants out of people on earth is a fundamental decency. The precepts in the holy books tell us how we're to conduct ourselves. They're uplifting, nice. They pretty much duplicate themselves in all of the texts. It's the distortions of some of these theologies that put the different sects at knifepoint. 'You have to believe this or you're an infidel and we may have to kill you because God tells us to.' Or, 'you have to be believe that Mary was a virgin or you're not a Christian.' Or, 'you have to believe Israelites are the chosen people or you're anti-Semitic and probably anti-Christian,' which is a real, industrial strength load to haul around."

"May I interrupt?"

"It would help."

"You're right about God wanting you to live a decent and generous life. But there has to be something a little more elongated than that. How do you live that life?

"I know there is. I'm starting with a simple premise. 'What does God will for me?' Getting older can work a lot of transformations in life but what it did in mine, sped by treatment for alcoholism, was to induce some working humility. When that quality is real, it disarms the magnetic power of that big and aggressive ME in life, and opens the window to the quiet and simple majesty of love. Romantic love was something that entranced me as a kid. One of the most memorable people I met in a lifetime of journalism was the late film star and dancer, Ginger Rogers. As a teen-ager I saw one of her movies, 'I'll Be Seeing You,' with Joseph Cotton and I could recite the title song lyrics almost word for word the rest of my life. They were that evocative to a moon-struck kid in northern Minnesota. At breakfast with her 25 years later, I told her about the movie and she teased me. 'I bet you remember the words to the song,' she said. I said I did. 'In that small café, the park across the way, the children's carousel, the chestnut tree'…and she finished, 'the wishing well.' Years later after she died, I wrote of that interlude and remembered her squeezing my shoulder as she left the table, and saying, 'I'll be seeing you.'

"Although I'd idealized love, I didn't really know how to express it and give it. I didn't because the center of my life for so many years was pretty much what I was doing, where I was going, my agendas, my thrills and who or what I was. While I was grappling with all that, I damaged or neglected some marvelous people who'd entered my life."

"What was there about love that you couldn't understand?"

"I hadn't exposed myself to the vulnerability of trying to give love unselfishly, or at least unselfishly within my capabilities to do that. The risk is that you will be a fool, that you can get hammered silly or simply that you have made an awesome mistake."

"What category did you finally occupy?" my interrogator asked.

"Ah, God, you are very nimble at repartee."

"I manage," God said modestly.

"I think I have now experienced this kind of love. Obviously it's not the same as bliss because for me love has brought with it a few spasms of turmoil and bafflement. I say that fondly. Relationships, even bolstered by love, can get loony, as you know. I think ultimately the core of wisdom in a relationship of love and mutual trust is what the French adventurer and writer, St. Exupery, said it is: "Love does not consist in gazing at each other but in looking outward together in the same direction.""

"And where," asked my interrogator, about to depart, *"do God and faith mesh in all of that."*

"When I've tried to understand how a renewed faith in God buoys my life, I have to tell myself what God *is* in my life and how I translate the presence of God in my life. For me, after I remove all of the ornaments, God is peace. God is the absence of fear. God is my companion in facing fear and turning it away. God is a refusal to hate. God is my protection against my own ignorance and folly. I really don't know if or where God greets me at the start of the day. All I can tell you is that I feel better when at the end of my small prayer in the morning I ask God to 'show me the way.'"

"So you believe God directs your life after all."

"No, I don't. I'm simply saying that I feel better knowing that I have said a prayer. I may die today or I may experience joy and excitement but I also want to say in that same breath, 'Thanks for the goodness in my life.'"

God's hand rested on the door latch. *"So we have come pretty much the full circle,"* he said.

I disagreed. "I have some final thoughts, and I wonder if you would have a few words for those."

He nodded.

"In a group I attended often, we would come around to a question: 'Is the world better today than it was 50 years ago, 100 years ago?' Often I took a minority position. The majority of my friends were relatively wealthy, although generous in the causes they supported and in their basic humanity. Most of them looked at social upheaval around the world, at the breakdown in parental influence, at casual violence in America. They saw the erosion of the institution of marriage, the vulgarity in entertainment and what one called 'the decline in civility.' And they concluded the world really is worse than it was.

"I thought differently. I said they were viewing the world as upper middle class or wealthy white Americans, appalled by the loosened codes of morality around them and the speed and random pandemonium of life today. I said that 50 years ago it was impossible for a person of color in America to seek or to be allowed to qualify for a job in business. In many places it was impossible for that person to vote, or to become a doctor or professor; or to dream of comfort and wealth reserved for the ruling white class. It was impossible for most women to dream of prestigious positions in business, politics or education. Girls were dismissed as cheerleaders in school. And people of color and in poverty around the world lived in the daily oppression of being first plundered and then ignored by the colonial powers.

"That," I said, "has changed for millions of people. And here in America we are closer than ever to fulfilling that loftiest visions of the founders of the country, of the great democracy, where people once considered intruders are now granted at least legal equality and are actually changing the face of America. And, women around the world are slowly gaining political and social power.

"And now I look at the world in the new millennium. And I have never seen ethnic and religious hatred and violence as we see it today. I see the gulf widening between those in power and those who are weak and voiceless. I see my own country sometimes acting and talking like the emperor of the world. There are significant parts of the world that have almost been forgotten, left to wallow in poverty, disease and tribal slaughter while the most powerful in the world quibble over trade policies and whose nuclear weapons are to be feared most, those of the powerful, the envious or the rogues. I don't see leadership and political bravery of the kind we saw in Gandhi, Martin Luther King, Harry Truman, Dwight Eisenhower, Anwar Sadat and Yitzhak Rabin. The world sees more chaos, and that is infuriating because it can still be, as the poet will tell us, a great and beautiful world."

God listened to this litany temperately.

"You know," he said, *"it's been worse. You and I started with you trying to draw a picture of what God means in the world and what God doesn't mean and what God, in fact, is all about. I may get into some trouble with self-ordained prophets about this, but I have to say: if you look in Scriptures for some guidance to the history of God, you're likely to get yourself into a hopeless swamp. The history of God in the texts has been transfused with myth and interpretations and re-interpretation, dreamed-up conversations between mortals and God, all stirred in with nationalistic goals and vendettas. I love the commitment of much that is in the Judaic and Christian Bibles and the Koran and, of course, in the writings from your Far East. But it's as though all of the great religious movements have conscripted God as an ally to give their ambitions and their philosophies of life the credibility they need, if not with the rest of the world, then with their own constituents.*

"I deplore that. I'd like to see a quieter worship than the clanging, podium-pounding perversion of worship that I see often. I don't doubt the sincerity of it. I do have some trouble with its goals and I have a lot of trouble with some of its arrogance, stupidity and actual cruelty.

"What I wish for the people on earth is so simple it is almost childish. It is to try to understand and to comfort and care for those around them, their neigh-

bors, people 10,000 miles away, people behind walls, people starving, shunned, infirm and people who simply need other people.

"Yes, create better understanding and desperately try to stop the killing. I know the cynics shout, 'Where is your God now?' If it's so monstrous and so evil, why doesn't God stop it?"

He paused and then said, "There is a God.

"And he will not stop it.

"It is humanity's world, to make as humanity will make it. There is the monstrosity of war and famine, hatred and revenge—in part because those who feel themselves deprived make demons of those with more and wage war or rebellion in their rage and futility. And those with more too often don't try to understand that there is another way to deal with those who have less, another way beyond ignoring them or exploiting them or leaving it to humanitarian volunteers to keep them from starving. So they give token food and sometimes token education. Ultimately, those who get those tokens begin killing themselves in tribal battles for power. They are not educated enough to govern themselves wisely and those who do govern usually can't resist corruption. And it's hideous. It is Africa and the Middle East and more."

I asked a question respectfully. "Are you a bystander, God?"

He might have been furious at that but he wasn't.

"I'm not a bystander. You suggested that the world seems to be on a terrible flight to chaos. And yet let me call your attention to the thousands of people in the place where you live, the hundreds of thousands of people, the millions of people in your country who give thousands of hours to the care and nurture of strangers, in your country and in countries half a world away. Multiply those numbers around the world. And now you have an immense gathering of human beings dedicated to the care of others. Some give their lives to it.

"Not all of these people are what you call 'believers.' But many millions are, and they are motivated by the most inspiring of all ideals—that they can help, and they will do it anonymously. That ideal is expressed in the Christian parable of the Good Samaritan. Most faiths have a comparable story. Its message is not hard to grasp: Be generous. Someone needs more than you do.

"That story is a lighthouse for human behavior. And in that story, God is not a bystander.

"God *is* the lighthouse?" I said.

"I don't think the lighthouse is there for the scenery. One clear and universal realization by people on earth might reverse the trend of this struggle between those who have and those who don't. If there is any basic right of humanity, it is for each human being to be given a chance to achieve all that his or her mind and heart are capable of achieving. You people call that utopian. If you don't mind, I call that the will of God. But there's one fundamental need

before any of this can begin to rise as the new house of peace in the world. And that is for people who live in countries where there is strength and wealth and comfortable living to understand something about all of those billions of poor. Being poor doesn't mean they don't have ambitions or dreams, that they won't work to realize those dreams. It doesn't mean they don't have good and creative minds. It simply means they are poor, born on arid land or in swarming cities where there is little hope. Give those people an incentive.

"Give them your friendship and your understanding as well as some of your money so they can make something of their lives. Think of them less as beneficiaries and more as partners in making a better world. And then let them work."

"It would be a start," he said. *"And it is already happening in some parts of the world."*

God was about to leave. *"I know you want something precise about who and what I am. I really can't give you that. It's what separates us, but that doesn't mean we can't love what the other means to us. And so we do. There is a political figure in America who I think summarized the exasperation of trying to define God, yet also the need to understand who God is. This is your Mario Cuomo of New York, who admitted it was hard to see the face of God or hear the voice of God in the hours of grief and tragedy, of a mother learning of the death of her son in war."*

> Cuomo said, that at those moments people weren't asking, "Who is God?" They were asking, "Is God?"

He went on: "For some of us the awful burden of living in a world without explanation was too much to live with. Our intellects pushed to find a rationale, an explanation, something larger than ourselves to believe in. If the answer could not be compelled by intellect, we pleaded for an answer that, at least, we could choose to believe without contradicting that intellect. It had to be more than just a God of prohibition. More than just a God of guilt and punishment...It had to be a God like the one that was promised in the ancient books: A God of mercy, a God of peace, a God of hope. In the end, to make any sense, it had to be a religion that God "so loved the world" that he made man. One that teaches the whole universe—even the pain and imperfection we see—is sacred; faith is not a call to escape the world, but to embrace it; creation is not an elaborate testing ground, but an invitation to join in the work of restoration. God created the world, but he did not finish it. He left that to us.

God pondered that thought and his eyes were full. *"It's the way it is and will be,"* he said, *"as long as there is earth, and human beings who are guided by their stars. By the way, what did you say was that expression of greeting in the Himalayas?"*

"Namaste," I said. "I praise the God who lives within you.

"That," he said, *"is the other way it is. We are together, you know. The pilgrim and God. Always."*

He opened the door, turned to me and said, *"I'd like you to go in peace, and I think we will meet again."*

The door closed soundlessly behind him.

Well, yes. Until we meet again. That is a reunion, I thought, to put in my appointment book.